Close Reading *and* Writing From Sources

Douglas Fisher
Nancy Frey

INTERNATIONAL
Reading Association
800 BARKSDALE ROAD, PO BOX 8139
NEWARK, DE 19714-8139, USA
www.reading.org

The International Reading Association attempts, through its publications, to provide a forum for a wide spectrum of opinions on reading. This policy permits divergent viewpoints without implying the endorsement of the Association.

Executive Editor, Publications   Shannon Fortner
Acquisitions Manager   Tori Mello Bachman
Managing Editors   Christina M. Lambert and Susanne Viscarra
Editorial Associate   Wendy Logan
Creative Services/Production Manager   Anette Schuetz
Design and Composition Associate   Lisa Kochel

Cover   Design, Lise Holliker Dykes; images, © Shutterstock/tanewpix, © Shutterstock/Mark Carrel, © Shutterstock/Seregam, © Shutterstock/Kostenko Maxim, © Shutterstock/Kampolz

The publisher would appreciate notification where errors occur so that they may be corrected in subsequent printings and/or editions.

Library of Congress Cataloging-in-Publication Data
Fisher, Douglas, 1965-
  Close reading and writing from sources / Douglas Fisher and Nancy Frey.
    pages cm
  Includes bibliographical references and index.
  ISBN 978-0-87207-158-2
  1. Reading (Secondary) 2. Reading comprehension. 3. English language--Composition and exercises--Study and teaching (Secondary) I. Frey, Nancy, 1959- II. Title.
  LB1632.F55 2014
  428.4071'2--dc23

                    2013049307

Suggested APA Reference
Fisher, D., & Frey, N. (2014). *Close reading and writing from sources*. Newark, DE: International Reading Association.

CONTENTS

Writing From Sources

Douglas Fisher, PhD, is a professor of education at San Diego State University (SDSU) and a teacher leader at Health Sciences High and Middle College in San Diego, California, USA. He received the Celebrate Literacy Award from the International Reading Association (IRA) and the Paul and Kate Farmer English Journal Writing Award from the National Council of Teachers of English and was a member of the SDSU teaching program that won the Christa McAuliffe Excellence in Teacher Education Award from the American Association of State Colleges and Universities in 2003. He has published numerous articles on reading and literacy, differentiated instruction, and curriculum design, as well as books, such as *Checking for Understanding: Formative Assessment Techniques for Your Classroom* (Association for Supervision and Curriculum Development [ASCD], 2007), *Better Learning Through Structured Teaching: A Framework for the Gradual Release of Responsibility* (ASCD, 2008), and *Enhancing RTI: How to Ensure Success With Effective Classroom Instruction and Intervention* (ASCD, 2010; all with Nancy) and *In a Reading State of Mind: Brain Research, Teacher Modeling, and Comprehension Instruction* (IRA, 2009) with Nancy and Diane Lapp. He can be reached at dfisher@mail.sdsu.edu.

Nancy Frey, PhD, is a professor of education at SDSU and a classroom teacher at Health Sciences High and Middle College. Before moving to San Diego, she was a special education teacher in Florida's Broward County Public Schools, where she taught students at the elementary and middle school levels. With Doug, she was also a member of the SDSU teaching program that won the Christa McAuliffe Excellence in Teacher Education Award in 2003. Nancy has served as the chair of IRA's Print Media Award Committee. Her research interests include reading and literacy, assessment, intervention, and curriculum design, and she was a finalist for IRA's Outstanding Dissertation of the Year Award. She has published in *The Reading Teacher, Journal of Adolescent & Adult Literacy, English Journal, Voices From the Middle, Middle School Journal, Remedial and Special Education, Educational Leadership,* and *California English.* She has coauthored books on literacy, such as *Improving Adolescent Literacy: Strategies at Work* (Allyn & Bacon, 2003), *Reading for Information in Elementary School: Content Literacy Strategies to Build Comprehension* (Allyn & Bacon, 2007), and *Scaffolded Writing Instruction: Teaching With a Gradual-Release Framework* (Scholastic, 2007; all with Doug). She teaches a variety of courses in SDSU's teacher-credentialing program on elementary and secondary reading instruction and literacy in content areas, classroom management, and supporting students with diverse learning needs. She can be reached at nfrey@mail.sdsu.edu.

INTRODUCTION

I f you've picked up this book, you are likely an educator who wants to guide students toward more effective reading and writing practices. You are probably thinking to yourself, What's new in this book? Or perhaps, What's different from what I am doing now? You might even be asking yourself if the information contained in this book is relevant to your teaching and to the needs of your students.

Before we go any further, let us say that we hope this book both validates and extends your instructional practices. We hope that there are some new things in this text that you may not have considered before. We also hope that there are some ideas and recommendations in this book that serve to reinforce your current practices. After all, teachers have been teaching students to read for a very long time. As a profession, we're pretty good at it and the vast majority of students learn to read. Does that mean that we reach all of the students or that we help them excel to their highest potential? Maybe not. But it does mean that there are some good practices that should not be thrown out as expectations for students are increased.

One of the wise practices that we hope is maintained as reading rigor is raised relates to purpose. Think of purpose as two sides of the same coin. On one side is the reader's purpose: *Why am I reading this? What do I want to get out of this text?* Before you read this text, you should know the answer to these questions. Similarly, your students should know the answer to these questions each time they participate in a reading-related lesson.

On the opposite side is the author's purpose: *What does the author want me to know? Why has this been written, and for whom?* A reader who can ascertain the author's purpose is able to begin to analyze the text. An author's purpose typically addresses one or more of the following:

- To entertain
- To persuade or argue
- To inform

You should also know the answer to these questions. It's probably fairly obvious that we hope to inform you about close reading and writing from sources; you could gather that from the title of the book. As you will see, we hope to persuade you to try some new instructional approaches, for example, annotations. Along the way, we might offer a bit of entertainment, especially as we relate stories from our own experiences. In addition to understanding their purposes for reading, your students should also develop an understanding of the author's purpose(s).

The RAND Reading Study Group (2002) identified determining the author's purpose as a key element of reading comprehension. The report notes that understanding the author's message is essential for determining the discourse structure, including

> text genre, the distinction between given (old) and new information in the discourse context, the points (main messages) that the author intends to convey, the topic structure, the pragmatic goals or plans of the communicative exchange, and the function of the speech acts (e.g., assertion, question, directive, evaluation). (p. 98)

With a clear understanding of the purpose in hand, students need to understand their task. Sometimes, their task is simply to read for pleasure. Other times, students need to read because they will be asked to synthesize information or produce ideas based on evidence. We limit our conversation in this book to tasks that require students to use evidence from the texts they read. This includes both discussions and written responses. Having said that, we recognize that there are other reasons to read and that the task demands can help students determine how carefully they should read. We hope that our attention to close reading and writing from sources does not crowd out aesthetic pleasure reading. Others have contributed excellent books about building students' reading habits through wide reading (e.g., Frey & Fisher, 2013; Pilgreen, 2000).

In this book, we hope to contribute to students' skills in reading closely to find out what the text says and means, and then to write convincingly from those sources. As part of this book, we have included video clips that can be accessed through QR codes or online via hyperlinks. These clips highlight a wide range of teachers' and students' perspectives on the information contained in the text. These middle and high school teachers represent math, science, social studies, English, and technical subjects. In addition to providing access to teachers' and students' thinking about the text, we introduce the big ideas in each chapter with a video. All of the videos in this book can be found on the International

Reading Association's YouTube channel: www.youtube.com/user/
InternationalReading. Additional classroom instructional videos
can be found on our own YouTube channel: www.youtube.com/
user/FisherandFrey. Access the video playlist at www.reading.org/
CRWFS or by scanning the QR code.

Returning to the content of this book, we are focused on helping
students read texts closely so that they can use that information in their
discussions and writing. We have developed, implemented, and refined
a process for teachers and students to use such that evidence becomes a
signature piece of their work. As noted in Figure i.1, locating evidence in a
text begins with framing an investigation, asking a question,
or identifying a problem to solve. Sometimes, this investigation or
question is presented as a prompt from the teacher. Other times, it is
based on something the reader—student—wants to know, prove, or
find out. One great place to find support for creating writing prompts
that demand evidence is the Literacy Design Collaborative (www
.literacydesigncollaborative.org). They have compiled a number of sample

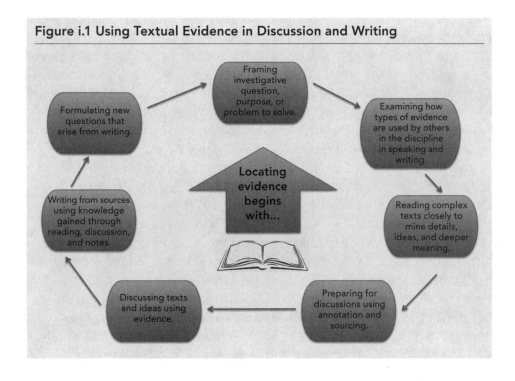

Figure i.1 Using Textual Evidence in Discussion and Writing

tasks, templates that teachers can use to construct tasks. All of their tasks ensure that students understand that evidence will be required. For example, after reading and discussing Chief Joseph's 1877 speech "I Will Fight No More Forever," students were asked to respond to the following prompt:

> What is the role of courage in surrender? After reading and discussing Chief Joseph's speech "I Will Fight No More Forever," write an essay that defines courage and explains the courageousness of Chief Joseph's decision. Support your discussion with evidence from the text. What conclusions can you draw?

Of course, students should have a lot of experience analyzing the various ways in which others use evidence. These others should include professional writers, teachers, and peers. For example, teachers can pause as they read a text aloud and note for their students how a particular author supplied evidence. Students can go on treasure hunts looking for evidence in the texts that they read. For example, students in David Crawford's biology class were asked to highlight evidence provided by authors of the texts that they read over the first month of school. One of the texts, a *New York Times* article about global climate change, provided students with an opportunity to examine how the author included statistics, references, and quotes. In addition, students can learn to analyze the arguments of their peers to determine when they include evidence. For example, when Yusuf was talking with Omar, he noticed that Omar was trying to convince him to try out for basketball. Yusuf said, "You're persuasive, but you haven't given me any evidence. You just keep telling me it will be tight. How do you know I would like it?"

Although learning from others is important, students have to develop habits that allow them to mine texts for details, ideas, and deeper meanings. In other words, they need to learn to read closely. Of course, that doesn't mean that they read everything with this level of attention, but that they learn when to read closely. When teaching students to read closely, the teacher has to create a series of questions that push students' thinking. For example, while reading Chief Joseph's speech, students were initially asked, "What concerns does Chief Joseph have about the health and welfare of his people? How do you know?" Of course, this question required that students look for evidence in the text. Importantly, this was not an end in and of itself. Instead, students were learning to find evidence; evidence that they could use later in their discussions and written responses. After reading and discussing the text several times, students were asked, "What is the tone of this speech? What words and phrases support your claim?" Again, they returned to the text to find out.

As part of the close reading students do, they hone their annotation and sourcing skills. For the most part, annotation has been left for college faculty to teach. It's rare for students to have sophisticated annotation systems in place during middle and high school. Unfortunately, this means that they often neglect to include evidence from the texts in their discussions or written compositions. Of course, students could return to the text again to find evidence, but often they simply do not. When they annotate as part of their close reading, they already have evidence identified and their job is to determine which pieces of evidence to use. Similarly, if they fail to identify sources, students run the risk of quoting or paraphrasing the work of others and then forgetting where it came from.

Understanding the purpose of and how others use evidence, reading closely looking for evidence, and annotating and sourcing texts are important aspects students must learn if they are going to be proficient composers who integrate evidence and respond to complex tasks. Unfortunately, it's not as simple as teaching these habits and skills. Students need time to interact with others to develop and deepen their understanding. Of course, there are summative tasks and assessments that students must complete individually, but learning how to do these things requires interactions with others. After all, learning is a social endeavor, not a solitary one. That's not to say that humans learn only in the presence of others. There is an important role that reflection and individual thinking time play in development. It's just that interaction opportunities—discussions—allow students an opportunity to adjust their thinking in real time. When they are pressed for evidence, offered counterclaims, or challenged by peers, their thinking becomes clearer. Over time, and with practice, they will begin to understand how others might respond to their ideas and evidence and begin to build a stronger case for their claims from the outset. In our experiences, setting aside time each day for students to discuss texts, using evidence from the texts they are reading, builds their thinking skills as well as their argumentation skills. That's why we include this aspect in our model—discussions are an effective link between reading and writing.

This brings us to the writing task itself. Students must be taught how to write from single sources and from multiple sources. They must learn to use the information they gathered during close reading and peer discussions in respond to the task at hand. They need to develop strong introductions, logical theses, and powerful voices. And importantly, these compositions will result in new questions that students want to investigate. These are often questions posed not by the teacher, but rather questions that students want to explore. For example, after reading and writing about Chief Joseph's speech, students wanted time to find out the answers to their questions:

- DeMarcus wanted to know what happened to the tribe after it surrendered.
- Myca wanted to know why there were reservations in the first place.
- Ernesto wanted to know if Chief Joseph committed suicide, having given up the sacred land where his father was buried.
- Alexis wanted to know if Chief Joseph found his people and if they were still alive.
- Gilbert wanted to know if the policies toward Native Americans were any more progressive now.

Isn't this what we want from our students? For them to become inquisitive learners who use their prowess to find out things that matter to them? The model that we have developed allows students to improve, both in terms of the habits they develop as well as in the products they create. Of course, this model is useless unless it is placed in the hands of good teachers.

Now it's up to you. You have to decide what's new and which aspects of our model will extend your practices and benefit your students. You have to decide which habits your students need. And you have to decide to create a classroom in which evidence is expected and ideas are valued.

CHAPTER 1

The Role of Evidence in Reading, Writing, and Discussion

Watch Doug introduce the chapter at www.reading.org/ch1_intro or scan the QR code.

Marcus and his group members have completed their reading of the introduction of *10 Days: Abraham Lincoln* by David Colbert as part of a classwide study of the 16th President of the United States. Other groups read different books about Lincoln, such as *Lincoln: A Photobiography* by Russell Freedman or *Lincoln: How Abraham Lincoln Ended Slavery in America* by Harold Holzer. Erin O'Malley met with each group, checking in on their reading and thinking. She asked Marcus's group to identify why Lincoln is seen as "the gold standard for a President, even today." Vincent answered first, saying, "Because of his ideas and vision for the country."

In the past, this correct answer would have been accepted, even without the student providing evidence to support his response. After all, the author says as much, just not in the same words. In too many classrooms of the past, correct answers did not require evidence; the teacher assumed that the student had evidence in mind. Unfortunately, student writing suggests otherwise. Far too often, students respond to writing prompts with no evidence in sight. It's recitation rather than reasoning.

When teachers do press for evidence, it's typically because the student has made an error or has a misconception. Too often, when a teacher asks a student for evidence, the student responds "Never mind," assuming he or she is wrong. This has to change. Students should not be surprised, or automatically think that they are wrong, when they are asked to supply evidence for their responses. Classrooms should be places in which evidence is expected. After all, it is expected in most other walks of life, from the courtroom to the boardroom, and lots of places in between.

Returning to the classroom learning about Lincoln, Ms. O'Malley knows that Vincent is on the right track. She also expects her students to supply evidence, in this case from the text itself. She asks the members of the group for evidence that supports or disputes Vincent's claim. Marcus answered, "Because it says right here that he helped create the world we now live in." Jennifer added, "The author says that he thought that the government should serve the people." Michael continued, "Yeah, it says that the government gets its power from the people, and we still think that today."

Making a Case for Evidence

Perhaps the first thing that comes to mind when you think of evidence is the kind that is presented in court. It is used to prove a claim and is often in the form of physical evidence or an eyewitness statement. The evidence may be circumstantial, which means that its presence can be explained in more than one way, or direct, and therefore in need of no further explanation. The jargon of the legal system punctuates our language: We speak of the *burden of proof*, and we turn to *expert witnesses* to help us with technical information.

Or maybe your orientation is of the scientific kind, and you consider evidence as the product of observation and experimentation. The scientific method requires that a hypothesis is proposed, and a fair test experiment is designed and implemented. The data are analyzed by the scientist, who draws conclusions that either support the hypothesis or show it to be false. The process itself is iterative in that proof of a false hypothesis guides the next round of inquiry.

Maybe neither of those orientations describes you at all. Perhaps you think of evidence in philosophical terms. You consider a claim ("It's the best movie of the year!") and consider the source (is it a friend with similar tastes, a respected film critic, or the movie's leading man?). You watch the trailer online and notice that the movie keeps coming up in conversations around you. Finally, you take a chance and decide to see it for yourself, knowing that you may or may not ultimately agree with the original claim but nonetheless acknowledge that the opinions of others are valid.

We've just described three kinds of evidence that are closely related but not identical to one another. Consider the legal example as the kind of evidence that builds an argument. The second, scientific evidence, rests on factual information to explain a process. Meanwhile, the third tells a story that is subjective in nature and may or may not be credible to you.

These types of evidence parallel the text types students read and produce in written and verbal forms. The National Assessment of Educational Progress uses different terms to describe the kinds of writing that students do. They write to persuade, explain, and convey experience (National Assessment Governing Board, 2010). These text types map onto the first three standards for writing in the Common Core:

1. Write arguments to support claims in an analysis of substantive topics or texts, using valid reasoning and relevant and sufficient evidence.

2. Write informative/explanatory texts to examine and convey complex ideas and information clearly and accurately through the effective selection, organization, and analysis of content.

3. Write narratives to develop real or imagined experiences or events using effective technique, well-chosen details, and well-structured event sequences. (National Governors Association Center for Best Practices [NGA Center] & Council of Chief State School Officers [CCSSO], 2010a, p. 18)

You may be in a region where the Common Core State Standards (CCSS) have been adopted; even if you aren't, the requirement to use evidence in writing predates them by centuries. Students also produce these text types in discourse as they offer and listen for the use of evidence in classroom discussions.

Watch Kim Elliott talking about the use of evidence at www.reading.org/ ch1_evidence or scan the QR code.

What Are Text Types and Why Do They Matter?

Text types are not synonymous with genres. Genres are a method of classification, such as *nonfiction, mystery, autobiography, speech, essay, business letter, brochure,* and so on. They allow us to group texts by *external* characteristics (Lee, 2001). These categorizations are useful for teachers in discussing the style and form in which a text is written. Text types, on the other hand, describe the *internal* characteristics of a text, especially the purpose. A recipe is a genre, while its text type is to explain a procedure. A debate is a genre, while its text type is to argue a position.

A police report is a genre; its text type is to convey an experience (Lee, 2001). Many genres are a combination of two or more text types, which are mixed and matched in countless ways. We read, we write, and we converse by sharing anecdotes, trading information, and attempting to persuade others to our way of seeing the world.

Students become more proficient at using and combining text types as they learn about organizational structures. Consider how younger and older writers report an event. Sanders and Schilperoord (2006) explain that younger students tend to rely on an action-line structure; that is, they recount an episode in chronological order or list a set of facts, which is produced primarily from drawing on episodic memory (*First I went to the pond and I saw a frog on a lily pad. Then it hopped to another one.*). Older students begin to use property-line structures that draw together a set of characteristics drawn from associative memory (*The green frog had long legs and was tan and spotted on its belly. The lily pads on the pond were a shiny dark green and floated on the water's surface.*).

Each has its strengths: Action-line accounts tend to have a clear organizational structure but not much detail, while property-line accounts have more detail but may lack organization; the researchers liken the latter to brainstorming. More sophisticated speakers and writers intermingle both action-line and property-line structures. "Text structure and discourse coherence…are constituting principles of text; without them, texts would be nothing but a random set of utterances" (Sanders & Schilperoord, 2006, p. 387).

In other words, we organize events, ideas, and arguments in a coherent fashion for a purpose and to meet the needs of an audience. Whether spoken, read, or written, these are organized into three kinds of text types: we convey experiences, we inform and explain, and we persuade (National Assessment Governing Board, 2010). Occasionally, only one text type is used by a speaker or writer; more often, two or more are interleaved to relay a coherent set of ideas using both action-line and property-line structures. Knowing the elements of each assists students in recognizing their use in the texts they read, discuss, and produce.

Conveying Experience, Real or Imagined

Mention writing and most will immediately think of narrative genres, either fictional or biographical. Narrative writing is linked most closely with novels, short stories, biography, autobiography, memoirs, and poems, as these genres usually consist entirely of one text type—conveying a real or imagined experience to the reader. However, this text type comprises a portion of so many other genres. For example, news accounts often begin by detailing the experience of an individual in order to put a human face on a widespread condition. Skilled writers are able to weave descriptions of the setting, the characters, their interior thoughts, and external dialogue in order to paint a vivid picture for the reader. Consider the opening paragraphs from *Bomb: The Race to Build—and Steal—the World's Most Dangerous Weapon* (Sheinkin, 2012):

> He had a few more minutes to destroy seventeen years of evidence.
>   Still in his pajamas, Harry Gold raced around his cluttered bedroom, pulling out desk drawers, tossing boxes out of the closet, and yanking books from the shelves. He was horrified. Everywhere he looked were incriminating papers—a plane ticket stub, a secret report, a letter from a fellow spy.
>   Gold ripped the paper to shreds, carried two fistfuls to the bathroom, shoved them into the toilet, and flushed. Then he ran back to his bedroom, grabbed the rest of the pile, and stumbled on slippers down the stairs to the cellar, where he pushed the stuff to the bottom of an overflowing garbage can.
>   The doorbell rang. (p. 1)

Can you feel the anxiety as Harry Gold frantically tries to dispose of evidence of his spying? And who is at the door? The author uses a narrative text type to convey the real experience of the unassuming chemist who passed on information about the Manhattan Project to the Soviets. The short sentences, tight dependent clauses, and use of punctuation make our hearts race as Gold's must have in the moments before the FBI agents arrived. The writer begins his book by capturing a memorable moment that sets the stage for discussion about Robert Oppenheimer, the physics of nuclear weaponry, and the political intrigue that marked the Cold War era. Although the genre of the book is expository nonfiction, it is laced with narrative text type passages such as this. Importantly, this passage serves the purpose of providing evidence to the reader of the situation Gold would soon find himself in.

We use narrative text types to convey our experiences in discussion as well. The family raconteur entertains others with a story of the escapades of two young boys, now grown men, at a family picnic held decades earlier. Nancy helps her grandchildren learn to make cookies by describing the way to gently stir the chocolate chips into the dough. Doug tells a story about a positive experience with a running shoe and uses it as evidence of his reasons for recommending the brand. We use narrative text types in our speech to entertain, inform, or persuade.

Characteristics of Narrative Text Types. Whether featured in a book, in a student's written work, or as part of a discussion, several elements mark this type of text as one that conveys an experience:

- Establish a context for the event, especially through the description of the setting, characters, and circumstances.
- Present the events using a logical sequence so the reader or listener can understand how it unfolds. Signal words and phrases are accurately used to help the reader or listener to understand the sequence and alert him or her when time shifts occur.
- Apply narrative techniques that suit the audience and the purpose, for instance using dialogue, moderating the pace, and furnishing descriptions that contribute to the reader's or listener's understanding of the event.
- Furnish a conclusion that matches the purpose of the narrative account so that the reader or listener can arrive at a similar conclusion.

Although these characteristics coincide with the Common Core writing standards, they are also helpful in considering how oral text is constructed, as well as how a reader understands a written text. Above all, effective speakers and writers construct narrative text when it aligns with the purpose, the audience, and the task. That is, it illustrates and illuminates a condition or idea by drawing on experiences that can be understood by others. Above all, it engages. As Ira Glass, host of NPR's radio show "This American Life," explains, the two building blocks of narrative are anecdotes that raise a question and moments of reflection to ponder them (watch the full interview at www.youtube.com/watch?v=loxJ3FtCJJA).

Learning About Narrative Text Types. In order for students to focus on how a writer crafts a text type, we ask students to engage in repeated dictation of a short spoken or written passage, no more than one paragraph in length. We read the passage aloud again and again so that students can accurately transcribe the message or play an audio recording of the text. What we don't do is allow them to simply copy it from a written source. They need to *listen* closely to how the writer or speaker builds the anecdote and poses the opportunity for reflection. Take this narrative passage from the short story "Salvador, Late or Early" (Cisneros, 1991):

> Salvador with eyes the color of caterpillar, Salvador of the crooked hair and crooked teeth, Salvador whose name the teacher cannot remember, is a boy who is no one's friend, runs along somewhere in that vague direction where homes are the color of bad weather, lives behind a raw wood doorway, shakes the sleepy brothers awake, ties their shoes, combs their hair with water, feeds them milk and cornflakes from a tin cup in the dim dark of the morning. (p. 10)

The repeated dictation exercise helps students focus on the writer's descriptive language, but it also raises questions. What is "the color of bad weather"? Why doesn't the teacher remember his name? What does Cisneros achieve by constructing an 80-word sentence? We usually have students read the sentence aloud to one another so they can experience the sense of breathlessness that the character feels through his hurried day. We sometimes use this process as part of a close reading of a complex text in order to scaffold student understanding about how the structure of a text matches the author's or speaker's purpose. By examining craft, students can begin to apply similar techniques to their own writing and discussion.

Informing and Explaining

A second text type is explanation to convey information. This is a dominant text type in secondary and postsecondary education, as it is built on a foundation of accuracy. Teachers routinely require the use of explanatory text types in writing and discussion in order to assess the extent to which a student is knowledgeable about a topic. For example, we pose a question about the requirements for moving a bill through legislation, and the student replies using an explanatory text type. Speakers, readers, and writers must draw on what they know about a topic, and in some cases investigate it further to gain new knowledge.

A number of genres feature explanatory text, especially procedural documents and manuals, essays, and summaries. Many of the verbs we associate with Bloom's taxonomy describe this text type: students use it to define, identify, label, list, demonstrate, and examine ideas, events, and phenomena. Topics primarily consist of those that are found in the biological, physical, and social worlds, including those that address scientific, political, and literary concerns.

Accuracy is paramount, and therefore what is shared must be crafted in such a way that it is clear for the reader or listener and does not strategically omit information that can lead them astray. Consider the author's explanation of deafness in *Far From the Tree: Parents, Children, and the Search for Identity*:

> More than a hundred genes for deafness have been identified, and another one seems to be picked up every month. Some kinds of deafness are caused by the interaction of multiple genes rather than a single one, and much deafness that occurs later in life is also genetic. At least 10 percent of our genes can affect hearing or ear structure, and other genes and environmental factors can determine how profound the deafness will be. About a fifth of genetic deafness is connected to dominant genes; the rest emerges when two carriers of recessive genes produce children together. (Solomon, 2012, pp. 60–61)

In these four sentences, the writer informs his readers about the complexity of congenital and acquired deafness, especially through his use of quantitative data to explain genetic expression and prevalence. But as is the case with so many informational texts, Solomon also uses narrative text types at other points in the book to spotlight families with a child who is deaf. These narrative and explanatory text types are interwoven to furnish evidence to support his main argument, namely that children who are unlike their parents face unique challenges in building identity.

Characteristics of Explanatory Text Types. We routinely use quantitative and qualitative evidence in explanatory text types by and arrange them in an order such that our audience (the listener or the reader) can understand them. These may be presented through discussion, as a visual display, or in written text. Explanatory text types require speakers and writers to do the following:

- Use accurate facts, provide examples, quote or paraphrase experts, and cite sources.

- Arrange these using one or more structures to compare and contrast, define and describe, link a cause to an effect, or propose a solution to a problem.

- Use language and vocabulary that matches the purpose, audience, and task, and signals when the speaker or writer is transitioning from one idea to the next.

- Provide a summary or conclusion to assist the listener or reader in retaining the information.

Learning About Explanatory Text Types. The issue of accuracy can be vexing for students, who often want to rely on what they already know (or think they know) rather than take the time to look at sources. "Oh *no*," they groan, "We have to do *research?*" Can't you just hear the collective whine as they slump down in their seats? We have frank discussions with students about the false sense of security that comes from believing you already know something, only to learn that (a) you were wrong, (b) you left out something really important, and (c) no one believes you. We have adapted an exercise suggested by McQuade and McQuade (2006) to make this point. We ask students to perform a simple task—to draw a penny from memory. "So *easy*," they think to themselves, and they happily draw away, delighted that they are doing something fun for a change instead of boring old English. After a few minutes, we pair them up to compare their drawings with others. "Wait a minute," they think to themselves, "how could that guy be so wrong?" Finally, we display the obverse and reverse sides (good vocabulary opportunity) of the coin on the document camera and ask them to write about the differences they observed between what they drew and the actual appearance. More importantly, we ask them to look for the moral of the story. Here's 10th grader Zenaida's response:

> I thought for sure I knew what a penny looked like! I've probably seen one every day of my life. I got the president right and I put a date on it, and I wrote "One Cent" on it. Boy, did I get it wrong! "One cent" is on the reverse. It says "In God We Trust" on the obverse, and the word "Liberty" is there, too. So here's what I think you want us to learn: Even when we're sure we know something, we have to do our fact checking.

Of course, one lesson in drawing a penny is not going to shift students' thinking about conducting research to prepare for discussions, reading, and writing. They have to be taught how to do it well and efficiently. But the use of evidence is elemental when seeking to explain and inform. It contributes mightily to voice and register as it aids in establishing a confident and authoritative tone. As we read and discuss complex text with students, we look for the organizational structures and methods writers use for presenting information. In turn, students use these same means to produce their own verbal and written products.

 Watch Kim Dinh talking about the importance of students being able to produce explanatory texts with a stats example at www.reading.org/ch1_explanatory or scan the QR code.

Persuading and Arguing

The purpose of this third text type used in verbal and written text is to persuade others regarding a "point of view, to take action, or to accept… [an] explanation or evaluation of a concept, issue, or problem" (NGA Center & CCSSO, 2010b, p. 23). The architects of the Common Core State Standards distinguish persuasive writing, such as the methods used in advertising and propaganda, from formal argumentation, as defined by Toulmin (1954). This model is used most often in secondary and postsecondary education to teach how a formal argument is crafted:

- *The claim* is the argument's conclusion you wish your listener or reader to agree with: *People with high blood pressure should make changes to their diet and activity levels to reduce the likelihood of heart attack or stroke.*

- *The grounds* include the facts, sources, and evidence that support your claim: *The Mayo Clinic states that high blood pressure over time damages arteries, the heart, and the brain. Lawes, Vander Hoorn, and Rodgers (2008) found that hypertension is responsible for over 7 million early deaths and 92 million disabilities.*

- *The warrant* links the grounds to the claim: *Lowered blood pressure among those who previously had high blood pressure lowered the rate of death for this group.*

- *The backing* is used to further support the warrant especially by invoking tradition, culture, history, or convention: *Although high blood pressure has been described as the "silent killer" because there are often no symptoms, public health campaigns have raised awareness and now more people than ever are being treated.*

- *The rebuttal,* sometimes called the *counterargument,* minimizes or dismisses claims that are in opposition to the one presented: *Long-term lifestyle changes are difficult to maintain, but with proper support can be successful.*

- *The qualifiers* limit the extent to which the claim should be applied: *When deemed necessary by a physician, statins should also be used. But their effectiveness is limited when no lifestyle change occurs.*

Figure 1.1 describes some of the differences between persuasive and argumentative texts.

In preparation for formal debates and essays, students can complete a table laying out their argument. This allows students and their teacher to examine the skeleton of the argument before all the other words obscure it from view. See Figure 1.2 for the argument graphic organizer 11th-grade student Yazmin completed to prepare for a debate in her health class.

Characteristics of Text Types That Argue a Position. The elements of argumentation are similar whether in oral or written forms:

- State a claim that is clear and address possible counterclaims.
- Cite evidence and examples to support the claim, using a structure that links the claim, the evidence, and the examples coherently.
- Remain objective as a speaker or writer and let the robustness of the reasoning used persuade listeners or readers.
- Use conclusions and summaries of evidence that allow the listener or reader to follow the line of reasoning.

Learning About Argument Text Types. We have found that classroom debates assist students in attending to the elements of argumentation. Debates are effective after students have closely read and discussed opposing pieces of text, often on a controversial issue. A debate is a problem task, requiring students to synthesize and analyze arguments

Figure 1.1 Differentiating Between Persuasion and Argument

The subtle, *but significant* differences between
Persuasive & Argumentative Writing

Persuasive Writing	V.	Argumentative Writing
The writer aims to get the reader to agree with him/his perspective.	**GOAL**	The writer aims to get the reader to accept his perspective/his side as truth.
Opinions are blended with facts, all in an attempt to convince the reader that the writer is "right."	**GENERAL TECHNIQUE**	Relevant reasons and credible data are blended to demonstrate the writer's argument as valid.
The writer needs an intended audience to address his request or need to. *Who can give him what he wants?*	**AUDIENCE**	To write an argument, the writer doesn't need an intended audience. The writer is satisfied with simply "putting the truth out there."
Since the writer is communicating directly to a person, group, or organization, it's common to use first-person (i.e., *I*) and second-person (i.e., *you*) point of view.	**POINT OF VIEW**	With no specific audience in mind, this more formal writing addresses the multiple sides of an issue using the more objective third-person point of view.
Persuasive writers "go after" their readers more aggressively. They consider the emotional strategy that will work best on their audience (e.g., manipulation, motivation, inspiration, etc.). Persuasive writing is personal, passionate, and emotional.	**ATTITUDE**	Argumentative writers maintain a tone of fairness and reasonableness. Their attitude is respectful, tactful, and formal.
Persuasion has a single-minded goal— *Get what the writer wants.* It is based on the writer's personal conviction that his way of thinking is the best. Consequently, the writer's viewpoint is typically the only one presented. (See the lopsided scales above.)	**PERSPECTIVES PRESENTED**	Argumentative writing acknowledges opposing views within a pro/con piece. (See the more balanced scales above.) This demonstrates the writer as a fair-minded person and gives him the opportunity to counter these perspectives with more logic, reasoning, and proof.
1. Pick a topic of interest. *(What do you want?)* 2. Choose a side to "fight" for. 3. Start writing.	**STARTING POINT**	1. Conduct initial research on a debatable topic. 2. Align with the strongest side. 3. Continue gathering facts and research.
Persuasive pieces rely almost solely on opinions and feelings. The writer uses his own passion and/or plays off reader emotions to get what he wants. The audience agrees with the writer because of strong emotional appeals.	**SUPPORT**	Arguments rely on logical reasons that are all substantiated by facts, data, expert quotes, and evidence. The audience agrees with the writer because of the strong logical appeals.

© 2012 **Smekens Education Solutions, Inc.** *www.SmekensEducation.com*

Note. Reprinted with permission from Smekens Education Solutions, Inc.

Figure 1.2 Yazmin's Elements of Argument Graphic Organizer

Element	Definition	Example
Claim	The assertion one intends to establish	Mandatory vaccination programs are necessary to protect the health of schoolchildren and the community at large. Those parents who raise moral, religious, and ethical objections should be required to meet with a physician to discuss the implications first.
Ground	Sources and facts that support the claim	Centers for Disease Control report a reduction in infectious diseases among populations with high vaccination rates. A herd immunity condition protects those who cannot be vaccinated.
Warrant	The way in which the data and the claim are connected	When vaccination rates have dropped, diseases like whooping cough and measles have rapidly risen. A mandatory vaccination program would reduce or eliminate these occurrences.
Backing	Cultural beliefs and historical traditions that further support the claim	Our society has a tradition of considering the common good when making decisions about the protection of an individual's rights and responsibilities. The common good is served when vaccination rates are high.
Rebuttal	The circumstances under which the claim would not be true or right	By making it easy for parents to decline vaccinations, the larger community is put at risk and the results can be disastrous.
Qualification	Setting the limitations for the claim	A small number of people should not be vaccinated due to a weakened immune system.

across texts. Teams of four students are organized in either support or opposition to a proposition.

For instance, students in Hilda Alvarado's 10th-grade world history class debated several propositions related to their study of World War II. One team's assigned proposition stated that the atomic bombing of Hiroshima and Nagasaki was justified because it ended the war with Japan. Each team revisited readings from the textbook, primary source documents, and historical accounts to develop an initial presentation. Importantly, their preparation also included anticipating what the other team might argue. On the day of the debate, the teams followed the accompanying schedule, while audience members and the teacher judged the soundness of the arguments:

Round 1: Initial Presentations
- Five-minute position presentation in favor of the proposal.
- Five-minute position presentation in opposition to the proposal.
    - Five-minute work period for both teams to prepare rebuttals.

Round 2: Rebuttals
- Three-minute rebuttal from the pro team.
- Three-minute rebuttal from the con team.
    - Three-minute work period for both teams to prepare responses.

Round 3: Response to Rebuttals
- Two-minute response to rebuttal from pro team.
- Two-minute response to rebuttal from con team.
    - Two-minute work period for both teams to prepare for summary statements.

Round 4: Summary of Position
- One-minute summary of position in favor of the proposition.
- One-minute summary of position opposing the proposition.

When the teams concluded, Ms. Alvarado reminded her students that they should vote on the validity of the arguments, not on one's personal support or rejection of the proposal. The feedback from their peers and Ms. Alvarado prepared students for their formal argumentative essays on the topic, especially in considering opposing views and addressing them through evidence.

Watch Heather Anderson talking about teaching debate and the importance of using evidence at www.reading.org/ch1_debate or scan the QR code.

The Intersection of Text Types for Discussion, Reading, and Writing

Our communication is intentional—we communicate to convey experience and learn about the experiences of others, to gain or explain information, to persuade others and to in turn be inspired to adopt a different point of view or be moved to take action. We can't parse our communicative lives according to speaking, listening, reading, writing, and viewing without losing the reciprocal and iterative effects that each has upon the other. Although the CCSS are categorized in this way, it is only to serve as a system of classification, not a syllabus for your course. Biological life doesn't exist as a taxonomy; birds live in the same biome as reptiles, amphibians, and mammals. The organizational structure of a taxonomy provides us with a common vocabulary for discussing a complex system. To continue the analogy, communication within the walls of the classroom is equally organic. The domains of the CCSS provide a way for us to talk about an equally complex system.

In similar fashion, the Core Standards for the English language arts intersect across text types. We use and combine these text types in a host of ways to achieve a purpose, fulfill a task, and communicate with an audience. A close look at the cross-cutting nature of the Reading, Writing, and Speaking and Listening standards reveals coherence across these domains. In Tables 1.1, 1.2, and 1.3, we have organized select standards according to text types to illuminate the integrated relationship between and among them. In addition, we have bolded key words and phrases that describe specific attributes of the text type.

The relationship between oral language, reading, and writing has been described by many researchers over the decades, but we especially like a phrase introduced by Bereiter and Scardamalia (1982), which reminds us that as teachers we should always be moving students "from conversation to composition" (p. 1). Students need to read about and discuss at length complex texts that can be mined for ideas and information, provoke reflection, and persuade through reasoning and logic. As part of what occurs between conversation and composition, we instruct students on the ways others have skillfully blended text types to achieve their purposes. And we need to ensure that students have occasion to write. Michael Graves challenges us to keep our students "in a constant state of composition" (cited in National Writing Project & Nagin, 2003, p. 23). We do so by ensuring that we read, discuss, and write about texts—print, digital, multimedia. And in doing so, we show students how others use evidence, how they can locate evidence, and how they can use evidence in their own verbal and written communication.

Table 1.1 Intersection of Standards for Argument

	Anchor Standards for Reading for Argumentation
1	Read closely to determine what the text says explicitly and to **make logical inferences** from it; cite specific textual evidence when writing or speaking **to support conclusions drawn from the text.**
3	Analyze how and why individuals, events, and ideas develop and interact over the course of a text.
8	Delineate and evaluate the argument and specific claims in a text, including the validity of the reasoning as well as the relevance and sufficiency of the evidence.
9	Analyze how two or more texts address similar themes or topics in order to build knowledge or to **compare the approaches the authors take.**
	Anchor Standards for Writing for Argumentation
1	Write arguments to support claims in an analysis of substantive topics or texts, using valid reasoning and relevant and sufficient evidence.
9	Draw evidence from literary or informational texts to support analysis, reflection, and research.
10	Write routinely over extended time frames (time for research, reflection, and revision) and shorter time frames (a single sitting or a day or two) for a range of tasks, purposes, and audience.

Pivotal Speaking and Listening Standards for Argumentation

	Anchor Standards for Speaking and Listening
1	Prepare for and participate effectively in a range of conversations and collaborations with diverse partners, building on others' ideas and expressing their own clearly and persuasively.
3	Evaluate a speaker's point of view, reasoning, and use of evidence and rhetoric.
4	Present information, findings, and supporting evidence such that listeners can follow the line of reasoning and the organization, development, and style are appropriate to task, purpose, and audience.
6	Adapt speech to a variety of contexts and communicative tasks, demonstrating command of formal English when indicated or appropriate.

Note. Bolded standards make specific reference to elements of argumentation.

How Is Evidence Used?

The use of evidence is not confined to writing. Readers look for evidence, logic, and reason to comprehend the texts they consume. Whether literary or informational, these elements provide a structure for readers to follow. Similarly, meaningful discussion is propelled by the use of evidence.

Table 1.2 Intersection of Standards for Informing and Explaining

	Anchor Standards for Reading for Information
1	Read closely to **determine what the text says explicitly** and to make logical inferences from it; cite **specific textual evidence** when writing or speaking to support conclusions drawn from the text.
2	**Determine central ideas** or themes of a text and analyze their development; **summarize the key supporting details and ideas.**
7	**Integrate** and evaluate **content** presented in diverse formats and media, including visually and quantitatively, as well as in words.
9	**Analyze how two or more texts address similar** themes or **topics** in order to **build knowledge** or to compare the approaches the authors take.
10	**Read and comprehend** complex literary and **informational texts** independently and proficiently.
	Anchor Standards for Writing to Inform
2	**Write informative/explanatory texts to examine and convey complex ideas and information clearly and accurately through the effective selection, organization, and analysis of content.**
7	**Conduct** short as well as more sustained **research projects** based on focused questions, demonstrating understanding of the subject under investigation.
8	**Gather relevant information** from multiple print and digital sources, assess the credibility and accuracy of each source, and integrate the information while avoiding plagiarism.
9	**Draw evidence** from literary or informational **texts to support** analysis, reflection, and **research**.
10	Write routinely over extended time frames (time for research, reflection, and revision) and shorter time frames (a single sitting or a day or two) for a range of tasks, purposes, and audience.

Pivotal Speaking and Listening Standards for Informing and Explaining

	Anchor Standards for Speaking and Listening
1	Prepare for and participate effectively in a range of conversations and collaborations with diverse partners, building on others' ideas and expressing their own clearly and persuasively.
3	**Evaluate a speaker's** point of view, reasoning, and **use of evidence** and rhetoric.
4	**Present information, findings, and supporting evidence** such that listeners can follow the line of reasoning and the organization, development, and style are appropriate to task, purpose, and audience.
6	Adapt speech to a variety of contexts and communicative tasks, demonstrating command of formal English when indicated or appropriate.

Note. Bolded standards make specific reference to elements of information and explanation.

Table 1.3 Intersection of Standards for Narration

	Anchor Standards for Reading Narrative
1	Read closely to determine what the text says explicitly and to make logical inferences from it; cite specific textual evidence when writing or speaking to support conclusions drawn from the text.
2	**Determine** central ideas or **themes of a text and analyze their development;** summarize the key supporting details and ideas.
7	Integrate and evaluate content presented in diverse formats and media, including visually and quantitatively, as well as in words.
9	**Analyze how two or more texts address similar themes** or topics in order to build knowledge or to compare the approaches the authors take.
10	Read and comprehend complex literary and informational texts independently and proficiently.
	Anchor Standards for Writing Narrative
3	**Write narratives to develop real or imagined experiences or events using effective techniques, well-chosen details, and well-structured event sequences.**
10	Write routinely over extended time frames (time for research, reflection, and revision) and shorter time frames (a single sitting or a day or two) for a range of tasks, purposes, and audience.

Pivotal Speaking and Listening Skills for Narration

	Anchor Standards for Speaking and Listening
1	Prepare for and participate effectively in a range of conversations and collaborations with diverse partners, building on others' ideas and expressing their own clearly and persuasively.
3	**Evaluate a speaker's point of view,** reasoning, and use of evidence and rhetoric.
4	**Present information,** findings, and supporting evidence **such that listeners can follow** the line of reasoning and the organization, development, and style are appropriate to task, purpose, and audience.
6	Adapt speech to a variety of contexts and communicative tasks, demonstrating command of formal English when indicated or appropriate.

Note. Bolded standards make specific reference to elements of narration.

A student states a claim and adds, "Because." Another student talks about a text and points to the sentence that transformed his understanding. A team of students engaged in a debate use information to support a line of reasoning. The use of evidence allows readers and listeners to understand.

In writing and discussion, evidence is described in terms of the larger form of discourse known as rhetoric. Because rhetorical principles matter, we ask young speakers and writers as they prepare: Who is your audience? What is your purpose? Rhetorical discourse provides a framework for telling a story to a theatergoer, explaining a procedure to an athlete, or persuading a listener on a podcast. According to Aristotle, rhetoric is "the ability, in each particular case, to see the available means of persuasion." He described three main forms of rhetoric: *ethos*, *logos*, and *pathos* (see Table 1.4):

- *Ethos*—Appeal based on the character of the speaker
- *Logos*—Appeal based on logic or reason
- *Pathos*—Appeal based on emotion

These appeals can be found in narrative, explanatory, and argument writing. Although "persuasive writing" is at times narrowly defined in some curricula, in truth virtually all writing is persuasive. In narrative writing, you are persuading the reader that a character's actions are plausible. Good explanatory writing is valued for its clarity and logical sequence of ideas. And of course argumentation writing relies on formal reasoning and logic. These same appeals are used in discussion in and out of the classroom.

Speakers and writers use an amalgam of appeals in order to persuade. Consider the remarks of Senator Robert F. Kennedy, who on the night of April 4, 1968, had to deliver the terrible news to a crowd that Dr. Martin Luther King, Jr. had been assassinated. His aides feared there would be

Table 1.4 Types of Appeals

Ethos	Logos	Pathos
• Language appropriate to audience and subject • Restrained, sincere, fair-minded presentation • Appropriate level of vocabulary	• Theoretical, abstract language • Literal and historical analogies • Definitions • Factual data and statistics • Quotations • Citations from experts and authorities • Informed opinions	• Vivid, concrete language • Emotionally loaded language • Connotative meanings • Emotional examples • Vivid descriptions • Narratives of emotional events • Emotional tone • Figurative language

a riot. But his impromptu speech used appeals of pathos in the form of empathy (Kennedy, 1968):

> For those of you who are Black—considering the evidence evidently is that there were White people who were responsible—you can be filled with bitterness, and with hatred, and a desire for revenge.

As well, his speech contained appeals of logos, using the work of the assassinated leader to reason:

> We can move in that direction as a country, in greater polarization—Black people amongst Blacks, and White amongst Whites, filled with hatred toward one another. Or we can make an effort, as Martin Luther King did, to understand, and to comprehend, and replace that violence, that stain of bloodshed that has spread across our land, with an effort to understand, compassion, and love.

Most memorably of all, he used the appeal of ethos, which links the speaker's credibility to the message. Robert Kennedy, who had rarely spoken publicly of his brother's death at the hand of an assassin, told the crowd:

> For those of you who are Black and are tempted to fill with—be filled with hatred and mistrust of the injustice of such an act, against all White people, I would only say that I can also feel in my own heart the same kind of feeling. I had a member of my family killed, but he was killed by a White man.

He ended this six-minute speech with a message that contained elements of all three:

> But the vast majority of White people and the vast majority of Black people in this country want to live together, want to improve the quality of our life, and want justice for all human beings that abide in our land. And let's dedicate ourselves to what the Greeks wrote so many years ago: to tame the savageness of man and make gentle the life of this world. Let us dedicate ourselves to that, and say a prayer for our country and for our people.

It's improbable that any of us will ever say anything that is that is still quoted more than 40 years later. But we all say and write things that influence our students, colleagues, and families. Our audience may differ from the one Kennedy addressed, but the need to tailor the message to the listener or reader remains. Consider a meeting Doug had with members of a ninth-grade team at a high school. Doug had been asked to work with the school because of low achievement and graduation rates. An analysis of the data illuminated several serious problems. Chief among them was the fact that 67% of the ninth graders at this school carried at least one F from the first marking period. When confronted with this data (*evidence*), the team went on the defense. "They come to us underprepared," one said. "We can't fight the effects of poverty on their learning," said another. "They just don't care," said a third.

Doug wanted teachers to commit to working with students and one another to build a positive school culture. He used an ethos appeal first, describing two successful students who had turned their academic lives around in a culture of caring (*evidence*). He moved on to a logos appeal, citing the research on increased student dropout rates among those with failing grades in the first months of high school (*evidence*). Using a pathos appeal, he reminded them of their commitment to education and asked them why they had chosen teaching as a profession (*evidence*). He concluded with another logos appeal, presenting a detailed plan used successfully at our high school to build a culture of achievement (*evidence*). It's hard to say which appeal did the trick; in all likelihood they affected each member differently. But in the end the team agreed that taking action was necessary. With that, the team settled in for the deeper discussion on how to make it work.

The Audience Shapes the Use of Evidence

Effective speakers and writers use evidence that matters to their audience. The match between audience and evidence is essential for communicating a message. Even the most humble messages are elevated when the audience and evidence align. Writer and high school English teacher Frank McCourt (2006) wrote about his experiences in the classroom in *Teacher Man: A Memoir*, admitting that in the early years of his career he was routinely disappointed by his students' lack of effort, as well as his own. He wrote of the day he reread their excuse notes piled up in a desk drawer:

> While my classes took a test that day I began to read notes I'd only glanced at before. I made two piles, one for the genuine notes written by mothers, the other for forgeries. The second was the larger pile, with writing that ranged from imaginative to lunatic.

I was having an epiphany. I always wondered what an epiphany would be like and now I knew. I wondered also why I'd never had this particular epiphany before.

Isn't it remarkable, I thought, how they resist any kind of writing assignment in class or at home. They whine and say they're busy and it's hard putting 200 words together on any subject. But when they forge these excuse notes, they're brilliant. Why? I have a drawer full of excuse notes that could be turned into anthology of Great American Excuses or Great American Lies. The drawer was filled with samples of American talent never mentioned in song, story or study. (McCourt, 2006, pp. 84–85)

Inspired by their forged notes, McCourt created a new series of writing assignments for his students—excuse notes from the famous and infamous. Excuse notes from Adam and Eve, from Al Capone. He even asked them to write an excuse note from the perspective of the parent of a teenager who is failing English. This creative writing assignment sparked students' interest, and they wrote with zeal.

But here's another analysis of the assignment. While McCourt says that he was simply attempting to engage his students in something—anything—we see also that this great writer was teaching them about the importance of the audience. Without an audience, speaking and writing wither. After all, why produce anything at all if no one is listening? When we teach about audience, we should also be talking about how understanding your listener or reader shapes the selection of evidence. We'll return to Doug's meeting with the ninth-grade team. He subsequently met with school administrators and the parent-teacher organization. In each case, his selection of evidence was influenced by the audience. The administrative team was interested in the nuts and bolts, while the parent-teacher organization wanted information on how it could support and extend the initiative. What's at work here is more than persuasion, at least the way it's conventionally taught. We've already stated that almost all communication is persuasive. What all effective communicators understand is how to match the audience with the evidence that will resonate with them.

Using Evidence Begins With Reading, and Lots of It

Texts underpin the use of evidence in discussion and writing. Students who are not widely read are constrained by the limited amount of text they have consumed and therefore have less evidence at the ready. We use the word *texts* as an umbrella term to describe the many sources of information available. At the forefront are those print and digital texts that convey experience, inform or explain, or argue a position. More broadly, the term includes networked information and communication technologies (ICT), which have had a growing influence on literacy instruction for 15 years. At the turn of the 21st century, Leu and Kinzer (2000) noted "rapid changes in ICT repeatedly alter the nature of literacy" (p. 117). This statement has become only more apparent in the ensuing years as ICT have taken on primacy in our own professional and true lives. In the same way that we use ICT to remain informed and current, so too must our students.

Texts, both print and digital, drive evidence. Some are seemingly timeless, as when consulting the writings of Galileo Galilei. However, even 500-year-old documents can be understood anew in light of more recent events, as when the Roman Catholic Church issued a 1992 declaration of apology for its opposition to his work. Access to a wide range of texts allows students to build knowledge. That in turn equips them with a growing storehouse of information and ideas to be used as evidence in discussion and writing.

The practice of using evidence in writing begins with learning how to use textual evidence in discussion. Close reading of complex texts builds the critical thinking habits necessary for students to move beyond a surface-level examination in order to locate its underlying structure and meaning (Fisher & Frey, 2013). The questions we pose to students about text determine whether they will dive deeper or skim the surface. For example, consider the following two questions that could be asked of readers studying the Declaration of Independence:

1. If you were present at the signing of the Declaration of Independence, what would you do?
2. What are the reasons listed in the preamble for supporting the authors' argument to separate from Great Britain?

The first question, perhaps an attempt to focus on the ethical decisions of the founding fathers, does not actually require that students read the document to respond. That's not to suggest that these types of questions are never asked, but rather that they are often asked prematurely, before a deeper and more nuanced understanding of the text has taken place. In order to gain that deeper understanding of the text, students are asked a number of questions that ensure their careful attention to it and what the author(s) offered.

The second question requires that students carefully consider the information presented in the text and provide evidence from the text in their responses. In addition, questions like this create a stronger conceptual foundation from which students can support their answers with specificity and detail. Knowing what you would do in a similar circumstance is vital, but making a difficult ethical decision requires knowing a great deal about the circumstances. The intent of such text-dependent questions during close reading is to build that foundation so that students can eventually answer the former using critical thinking, not just vague and unsupported claims.

 Watch students engaged in discussion based on text-dependent questions at www.reading.org/ch1_questions or scan the QR code.

Close reading, which is discussed in detail in Chapter 2, scaffolds the habit of using evidence in several important ways:

- Supports deep comprehension by explicitly locating the textual evidence under discussion
- Slows the reader down in order to continuously engage with the author
- Promotes intellectual discourse
- Teaches students how writers use evidence
- Builds awareness of what their audiences need from them as speakers and writers

In other words, close reading helps to develop students' abilities to regularly apply the habits of critical thinking. But discussion of complex texts should not be limited to regurgitation and recitation of the text in front of them. It is necessary, but not sufficient, to form a literal understanding of the text. But without analysis, debate, evaluation, and interpretation, *Moby-Dick* is nothing more than a hunt for a white whale.

With the habit of locating evidence in texts comes an appreciation of what their own readers and listeners require of them. Close reading gets students "paying attention to the decisions a writer makes" (Newkirk, 2011, p. 2). They witness how skilled writers incorporate statistics and visual displays of quantitative information into informational and argumentative text types. Students discover how well-constructed summaries help readers frame their understanding of a complex text. They notice how characters, plot points, and details are interwoven to form a cohesive fabric of story. They can even learn how and why direct quotations are used, whether in support of a stance, to capture a memorable turn of phrase, or to separate one's own position from that of another writer (Spatt, 2011). Depending on the discipline, they may also be learning to consider the source of information.

Considering the Source of the Evidence

Wineburg's (1991) comparative study of the cognitive practices of high school history students and historians found that one practice in particular separated the two groups: the ability to source the information in order to properly contextualize what was being read. Sourcing is fundamental for historical interpretation and analysis, as it can expose the bias of the writer. Closely related to sourcing is corroboration; that is, whether the account of a historical event is anecdotal or can be validated through other sources. Although the concepts of sourcing and corroboration are associated with historical thinking, they can be applied to the use of evidence in other disciplines as well.

Students across the disciplines find themselves reading primary sources of information written close to the time in which an event occurred. In history, these include newspaper articles, letters and diaries, maps, and other documents that are first-hand accounts. Secondary sources are those that were developed after the event in question, where the author had no direct knowledge. These can include biographies of deceased individuals and films of historical events. Tertiary sources are those that are compiled, such as history textbooks. The sciences define these somewhat differently, with published research accounting for primary sources, reviews and commentary composing secondary sources, and reference and textbooks considered tertiary.

More broadly, we try to get students to regularly analyze sources, be they primary or tertiary, using a framework for thinking through the sources of evidence they use. The CARS framework, developed by Harris (2010), is useful for considering information provided (see Table 1.5). Although Harris developed CARS with Internet sources in mind, we have found it to be equally sound for discussing print sources.

Similarly, Zhang, Duke, and Jiménez (2011) developed a system for teaching students to think about sources of information. Like Harris, they focused on Internet sources, and we have found it to be useful with a wide range of print and digital texts. Also like Harris, they use a mnemonic, but theirs is WWWDOT, in which students are taught to think about:

- *W*ho wrote this and what credentials do they have?
- *W*hy was it written?
- *W*hen was it written and updated?
- *D*oes this help meet my needs (and how)?
- *O*rganization of website?
- *T*o-do list for the future (such as finding additional sources, corroborating information with other sources, asking questions of others, or sharing information with family members or friends).

Table 1.5 Summary of the CARS Checklist for Research Source Evaluation

Credibility	Trustworthy source, author's credentials, evidence of quality control, known or respected authority, organizational support. Goal: an authoritative source, a source that supplies some good evidence that allows you to trust it.
Accuracy	Up-to-date, factual, detailed, exact, comprehensive, audience and purpose reflect intentions of completeness and accuracy. Goal: a source that is correct today (not yesterday), a source that gives the whole truth.
Reasonableness	Fair, balanced, objective, reasoned, no conflict of interest, absence of fallacies or slanted tone. Goal: a source that engages the subject thoughtfully and reasonably, concerned with the truth.
Support	Listed sources, contact information, available corroboration, claims supported, documentation supplied. Goal: a source that provides convincing evidence for the claims made, a source you can triangulate (find at least two other sources that support it).

Note. From "Evaluating Internet Research Sources," by R. Harris, 2010, *VirtualSalt*. Retrieved from www.virtualsalt.com/evalu8it.htm. Reprinted with permission.

Conclusion

It isn't enough to routinely settle for an answer without evidence, any more than it would be expected that a student could write a research paper without using credible sources. Yet students often have little practice in furnishing evidence outside of formal written assignments. One barrier to student use of evidence is that they have limited practice in seeing how evidence is used in discussion and in the texts they read. A focus on text types—narrative, informational, and argumentative—provides students with a means for noticing how skilled speakers and writers use evidence. That intersection of literacies, especially speaking, reading, and writing, can further build students' capacity to locate and use evidence for a variety of purposes. In the next chapter, we explore how close reading can be leveraged to teach students about the use of evidence.

CHAPTER 2

Close Reading of Complex Texts

 Watch Nancy introduce the chapter at www.reading.org/ch2_intro or scan the QR code.

Deep understanding, and writing in response to that understanding, begins with close reading and discussion of texts. In other words, students have to actually understand what the author said, whether they agree with the author. They also have to be able to use information from the texts that they have read in support of the points they want to make, whether that be to argue a perspective, inform or explain, or to convey an experience. This does not mean that students must ignore their own experiences or beliefs, but rather that they "must remain faithful to the author's text and must be alert to the potential clues concerning character and motive" (Rosenblatt, 1995, p. 11). Rosenblatt cautioned that otherwise readers might ignore elements in a text they did not agree with or did not understand, thus failing to realize that they are "imputing to the author views unjustified by the text" (p. 11).

Text is an important source for building academic knowledge. In turn, students draw on a strong foundation of knowledge to provide evidence in their discussions and writing. Yet teachers are faced with a conundrum: How can complex texts be used when so many students are not able to read them on their own? This has led to a decades-long reduction in the complexity of texts students consume (Hayes, Wolfer, & Wolfe, 1996) as teachers attempted to supplement the information through other instructional practices. But it can be argued that an overreliance on text-free instruction results in students who don't know how to locate textual evidence because they don't have enough opportunities to do so. As noted in the CCSS:

> Being able to read complex text independently and proficiently is essential for high achievement in college and the workplace and important in numerous life tasks. Moreover, current trends suggest that if students cannot

read challenging texts with understanding—if they have not developed the skill, concentration, and stamina to read such texts—they will read less in general. In particular, if students cannot read complex expository text to gain information, they will likely turn to text-free or text-light sources, such as video, podcasts, and tweets. These sources, while not without value, cannot capture the nuance, subtlety, depth, or breadth of ideas developed through complex text. (NGA Center & CCSSO, 2010b, p. 4)

Close reading is an instructional practice that makes complex texts accessible using repeated reading, cognitive scaffolding, and discussion. All three of these conditions are vital in order for students to understand complex texts and build the habits needed for deep comprehension. Keep in mind that the instruction about a piece of text is slowed down in order for students to read and revisit it over several lessons. We like a path that guides students through multiple encounters with the text, generally organized around three questions: *What does the text say? How does the text work? What does the text mean?*

It is essential to note that increasing students' ability to read complex texts should not be misinterpreted as "pass and pray"—in other words, pass out hard books and pray for the best. As Allington (2002) noted, "You can't learn much from books you can't read" (p. 16). In order to steadily build students' capacity for comprehending complex texts, teachers must carefully scaffold reading experiences. This begins with text selection. Some texts are not complex enough to warrant close reading. That doesn't mean that they are bad texts, but rather that they do not require the level of investigation and interrogation that is the focus of this chapter. In Common Core language, teachers must determine which texts should be used in teacher-led learning activities such as close reading versus those that can be used in peer-led learning activities or independent tasks. Again, text selection is critical.

> *Watch student Emily talking about close reading at www.reading.org/ch2_close1 or scan the QR code.*

Selecting Complex Texts

Observe people at a bookstore or library and you'll get an idea of the array of techniques they use to size up a text to determine if it's right for them.

Some will read the back cover or fan the pages to eye the font size. Others will turn the book sideways to see how thick it is. Some will turn to the table of contents or the index to gain a sense of its contents. A smaller proportion will read the introduction in an effort to decide whether it meets their needs. These techniques, however informal, encapsulate the array of tools used to determine the complexity of a text. These include quantitative measures related to the words and sentences, the qualitative factors surrounding the content, the unique characteristics of the reader, and the task or purpose for reading.

Quantitative Factors

One way to think about text complexity centers on aspects of the text that can be quantified, typically by a computer. Most quantitative readability formulas, including familiar ones such as the Fry (2002), the Dale-Chall (1995), and the Flesch-Kincaid (1948), rely on varying algorithms that factor word length and frequency of use in English, number of syllables, and sentence length. Even newer readability formulas, such as those used by Lexile (Smith, Stenner, Horabin, & Smith, 1989) and Degrees of Reading Power (Koslin, Zeno, & Koslin, 1987) rely on these relatively straightforward methods of measuring text. However, these formulas measure the surface qualities of a text and do not provide information about the content or the way in which the ideas that are built across the text hang together, a factor called coherence.

Most teachers have learned through experience that quantitative factors, while informative, do not go far enough to provide the kind of guidance needed to select text. "I remember my first year of teaching. I was at the middle school," said seventh-grade social studies teacher Mae-Ling Yung. She continued,

> I had to set up my classroom pretty quickly, so I went to the bookroom at the school and just started pulling books that said "Grade 7" on the spine. But as I started using them, I realized that some were much too easy for my students, while others were just ridiculously difficult. I learned my lesson that year—I need to read it to figure out whether it's right for us.

Ms. Yung's frustration with her method of selecting texts highlights the limitations of relying on only one element of a text's characteristics: ignore content, the reader, and the task at one's own peril. Those who advocate for the use of readability formulas like those mentioned earlier also provide a similar caution and advise that quantitative measures should be used to initially screen a text, but only in conjunction with other ways of assessing a text's suitability (Gunning, 2003). The qualitative factors related to content, levels of meaning and purpose, text structure and organization, and even the presence of visual supports, contribute to a text's complexity.

Qualitative Factors

The appeal of quantitative factors is in the ease of calculation, made all the more efficient through the use of computers and digital texts. But qualitative measures need a human being to assess them; they can't be measured in the same way as quantitative methods allow for (NGA Center & CCSSO, 2010b). Qualitative factors include content analysis, levels of meaning and purpose, text structure and organization, visual supports, and knowledge demand.

Content Analysis. While the readability measure on a text may be relatively low, the content can be quite challenging. One of our favorite examples is Kurt Vonnegut's (1998) *Cat's Cradle*. The author's unique style using short sentences punctuated by longer ones, as well as lots of dialogue and poetry, results in an elementary-level readability. But the science fiction novel's deeply satirical commentary on war, the coming apocalypse, and spies would elude a child, and in fact would challenge older children as well.

Watch Marisol Thayre talking about selecting texts at www.reading.org/ch2_text or scan the QR code.

Levels of Meaning and Purpose. We'll use Vonnegut's novel again to illustrate this factor. On the surface, the novel is an entertaining tale about a chase for a valuable substance that can turn water solid at room temperature. But its reputation as one of the most important novels of the 20th century is not due to the author's ability to weave a good yarn. Vonnegut likely had more subversive intentions when he wrote the book, especially in offering biting commentary on the roles of religion and technology in a society. Without an understanding of the time it was published (at the height of the Cold War) and its references to historical events, including the development of the atomic bomb and the bombing of Hiroshima and Nagasaki, a reader would not discern the author's more subtle messages.

Text Structures and Organization. Texts use structures that allow the reader to follow a plot (narrative), gain information (informational), or be persuaded (argumentative). These structures provide an organizational frame for the use of one or more text types to propose a solution to a problem, describe a sequence, link a cause to an effect, or compare and contrast two concepts. Some genres use specialized ones such as dramatic structure (exposition, rising and falling action, climax, and denouement) or poetic structures (foot, meter, rhythm, line). Texts are generally a bit easier to read when they include more signal words that alert the reader to a structure, such as *first, next,* and *finally* in a chronologically ordered text. You'll recall from the previous chapter that younger students often rely on this approach (action-line) in their writing and speech. The presence of organizational features such as headings and subheadings make the reading easier.

Visual Supports. It isn't the mere presence or absence of visual supports like photographs, diagrams, and charts that makes a text more or less difficult. If it were, we could simply flip through the pages of a book to count the pictures and then be done with it. But visual supports that are closely tied to the main part of the text can be helpful. For example, a science passage on the rock cycle can become easier to understand if accompanied by a clear, accurate illustration that closely aligns with what is offered in the text. If, however, the same great illustration is only briefly referred to in the passage, it is less helpful. Conversely, an ill-designed chart in a social studies textbook can make the main part of the text more confusing, not less.

Knowledge Demands. Texts are written for different audiences and presume a certain level of the reader's knowledge going in. Texts that provide examples, embedded definitions, and extended descriptions are usually a bit easier to understand than those that assume high levels of prior knowledge on the part of the reader.

Just as a qualitative examination of a text to determine its appropriateness requires an expert eye, so too does inspection of the reader. Each student brings strengths and areas of need to a text, and these variables further influence his or her understanding of it. These factors specific to the reader include language proficiency, background knowledge and experiences, and level of motivation.

The Reader

Every time we read, we bring a host of experiences, knowledge, and opinions to the text. In turn, the text acts upon us as we read to further evoke and inform those experiences. Rosenblatt (1938/1978) called this *transaction* and noted that the reciprocal relationship between the reader and the text influences its understanding. Although widely accepted today, it was a revolutionary stance in the early 20th century, when the primary role of the reader was limited to correctly interpreting what the author meant. These unique factors, once believed to be unimportant, have taken center stage in the ensuing decades. Today, it would be unthinkable to fail to consider language, knowledge, experiential, and motivational factors when considering a text.

Language Proficiency Factors. Students identified as English learners do additional cognitive work as they must attend both to the message of the text and the necessary cognitive resources needed to make sense of a text written in a less familiar language. In similar fashion, students with learning or reading disabilities must use compensatory resources to process text efficiently. We find it helpful to think of all our students as language learners; that is, learners of the language of the discipline. All readers must tackle unfamiliar vocabulary, text types, and rhetorical structures that can make a text more difficult.

The Reader's Experiences and Knowledge. Variance in experiences may include economic, social, familial, and individual factors and are undoubtedly present in every classroom. When it comes to a reading, these experiences should be taken into account. These may involve the whole class, as in U.S. history, where virtually every student lacks the experience of a society without child labor laws, and therefore can't draw on this to understand the need for legal changes in the Progressive Era.

At other times, it is situational, as with a student whose own life experiences have not adequately prepared him or her to understand the familial responsibilities felt by Tom Joad in John Steinbeck's *The Grapes of Wrath*.

The Reader's Motivation. The intrinsic interest a reader brings to a text can make it accessible in ways that defy conventional measures of ability. We recall a time when one of our students, a survivor of political persecution in an African nation, devoured Ishmael Beah's *A Long Way Gone: Memoirs of a Boy Soldier*. His motivation to read an autobiographical recounting of forced conscription in Sierra Leone's civil war trumped his nascent skills as an English learner. It is also likely that his experiences provided him with a deeper understanding of the author's message.

The quantitative and qualitative measures of a text, as well as the characteristics of the reader, must be taken into consideration when selecting a complex piece. These factors should further inform the design of the task itself. After all, a text is just ink on a page (or an image on a screen) until a reader interacts with it. These interactions are realized through the tasks we design.

The Task

Reading complex texts should not be a private affair—it should be punctuated with teacher modeling and think-alouds, collaborative learning in the company of peers, and discussion propelled through text-based questions.

Teacher-Led Tasks. These provide students with insight into how the text is understood by an expert in the discipline (you!). This is accomplished through modeling, especially when students, after reading the passage themselves, get to hear how you read the text. Prosodic reading, the smooth, fluent, and expressive oral reading of a text, promotes comprehension for students. They get to hear how you pronounce words, use phrase boundaries, and apply intonation as an active reader who is making meaning while reading. Of course, this is much more effective when you have read the passage several times in advance. In addition, think-alouds (Davey, 1983) give students insight into how you use your background knowledge, resolve problems when comprehension breaks down, or solve an unfamiliar word or phrase. Close reading instruction often includes teacher modeling and think-alouds so that students can grow in their metacognitive awareness. In addition, the teacher guides the discussion using text-dependent questions.

Peer-Led Tasks. These offer students the opportunity to further clarify their understanding of complex text. Simple instructional routines such as Think-Pair-Square (Kagan, Kagan, & Kagan, 1997) allow students to discuss the text first with a partner, then with another pair of students as a group of four. Of course, the conversation needs to have parameters so that it is an enriching experience and not merely a chance to socialize for a few minutes. By teaching discussion-based strategies such as accountable talk (Michaels, O'Connor, & Resnick, 2008), students can learn to apply elements of argumentation in order to reach deeper levels of understanding in the company of peers. Texts chosen for peer-led tasks are usually somewhat less complex than those selected for close reading. They should be challenging enough that students have reason to discuss the text with others. Two examples of peer-led tasks are reciprocal teaching (Palincsar & Brown, 1984) and literature circles (Daniels, 2002).

Independent Reading Tasks. These provide less in the way of formal supports as students make their way through texts largely on their own. Independent reading in and out of the classroom is a cornerstone for building knowledge. However, it should not be lost in the rush to use complex texts that reading for pleasure—for its own intrinsic rewards—is essential. Students need ample opportunities to read widely, to read what they choose (not just what is assigned), to read at their own pace, and to read for their own purposes. Reading can be transformative (Ivey & Johnston, 2013). We stated that independent reading tasks often have little formal support. But the informal support that comes from talking with an engaged adult about reading is invaluable and builds a classroom community.

> *Watch student Yusuf talking about close reading at www.reading.org/ch2_close2 or scan the QR code.*

Building Capacity Through Close Reading

The practice of close reading is not a new one, and in fact has existed for many decades as the practice of reading a text for a level of detail not used in everyday reading. The purposes are to build the habits of readers as they engage with the complex texts of the discipline and to build their stamina and skills for being able to do so independently. However, it is important to note that close reading doesn't mean that you simply distribute a complex reading and then exhort students to read it again and again until they understand it. Instead, close reading should be accompanied by purposeful, scaffolded instruction about the passage. A vertical progression from grades 6–12 for Reading Standard 10 in English language arts, history, science, and the technical subjects appears in Table 2.1.

Select Short, Worthy Passages

Because close readings can be time-consuming, it is often best to select shorter pieces of text for instruction. In Figure 2.1 and Figure 2.2, you will find two short pieces from General Dwight D. Eisenhower, both written just before the launch of the D-Day operation in June 1944. (Digital images of these primary source documents can be retrieved at ourdocuments.gov/doc.php?flash=true&doc=75 and www.archives.gov/education/lessons/d-day-message/, respectively.) U.S. history teacher Melissa West selected both of these for a close reading so her students could better understand the uncertainty of success and the risk of failure. "I want them to see that leadership in war is extraordinarily difficult, and that our historical 'rear-view mirror' glances don't always let us see the contemporary issues of the day," she said. She selected the letter General Eisenhower wrote to the Allied troops as they embarked on this mission. But tellingly, he also drafted a message to be delivered in the event the operation failed.

Design the Lesson So Students Reread

"These two readings are not very long, and I know their tendency is going to be to read them quickly and move on," Ms. West said. "I want to make sure they stay with these two readings and take the time to compare the differences in the messages." Therefore she designed the overall lesson to encourage students to read the texts several times. "I prepare my questions in advance so I can remember to ask them for information they need from the reading," she said. In addition, she constructed a series of tasks that require students to read the messages at least three times.

Table 2.1 Vertical Progression of Reading Standard 10

	Reading: Literature and Informational Texts Range of Reading and Level of Text Complexity	
	**CCR Anchor Standard 10:** Read and comprehend complex literary and informational texts independently and proficiently.	
Grade	**Grade-Specific Standard**	
Grade 6	By the end of the year, read and comprehend literature, including stories, dramas, and poems, and literary nonfiction in the grades 6–8 text complexity band proficiently, with scaffolding as needed at the high end of the range.	
Grade 7	By the end of the year, read and comprehend literature, including stories, dramas, and poems, and literary nonfiction in the grades 6–8 text complexity band proficiently, with scaffolding as needed at the high end of the range.	
Grade 8	By the end of the year, read and comprehend literature, including stories, dramas, and poems, and literary nonfiction at the high end of grades 6–8 text complexity band independently and proficiently.	
Grades 9–10	By the end of grade 9, read and comprehend literature, including stories, dramas, and poems, and literary nonfiction in the grades 9–10 text complexity band proficiently, with scaffolding as needed at the high end of the range. By the end of grade 10, read and comprehend literature, including stories, dramas, and poems, and literary nonfiction at the high end of the grades 9–10 text complexity band independently and proficiently.	
Grades 11–12	By the end of grade 11, read and comprehend literature, including stories, dramas, and poems, and literary nonfiction in the grades 11–CCR text complexity band proficiently, with scaffolding as needed at the high end of the range. By the end of grade 12, read and comprehend literature, including stories, dramas, and poems, and literary nonfiction at the high end of the grades 11–CCR text complexity band independently and proficiently.	

	Literacy in History/Social Studies Range of Reading and Level of Text Complexity	
	**CCR Anchor Standard 10:** Read and comprehend complex literary and informational texts independently and proficiently.	
Grade	**Grade-Band Standard**	
Grades 6–8	By the end of grade 8, read and comprehend history/social studies texts in the grades 6–8 text complexity band independently and proficiently.	
Grades 9–10	By the end of grade 10, read and comprehend history/social studies texts in the grades 9–10 text complexity band independently and proficiently.	
Grades 11–12	By the end of grade 12, read and comprehend history/social studies texts in the grades 11–CCR text complexity band independently and proficiently.	

(continued)

Table 2.1 Vertical Progression of Reading Standard 10 (continued)

Literacy in Science and Technical Subjects Range of Reading and Level of Text Complexity	
CCR Anchor Standard 10: Read and comprehend complex literary and informational texts independently and proficiently.	
Grade	Grade-Band Standard
Grades 6–8	By the end of grade 8, read and comprehend science/technical texts in the grades 6–8 text complexity band independently and proficiently.
Grades 9–10	By the end of grade 10, read and comprehend science/technical texts in the grades 9–10 text complexity band independently and proficiently.
Grades 11–12	By the end of grade 12, read and comprehend science/technical texts in the grades 11–CCR text complexity band independently and proficiently.

Figure 2.1 General Dwight D. Eisenhower's D-Day Invasion Statement to Troops

June 6, 1944

Soldiers, Sailors and Airmen of the Allied Expeditionary Force!

You are about to embark upon the Great Crusade, toward which we have striven these many months. The eyes of the world are upon you. The hopes and prayers of liberty-loving people everywhere march with you. In company with our brave Allies and brothers-in-arms on other Fronts, you will bring about the destruction of the German war machine, the elimination of Nazi tyranny over the oppressed peoples of Europe, and security for ourselves in a free world. Your task will not be an easy one. Your enemy is well trained, well equipped and battle hardened. He will fight savagely. But this is the year 1944! Much has happened since the Nazi triumphs of 1940-41. The United Nations have inflicted upon the Germans great defeats, in open battle, man-to-man. Our air offensive has seriously reduced their strength in the air and their capacity to wage war on the ground. Our Home Fronts have given us an overwhelming superiority in weapons and munitions of war, and placed at our disposal great reserves of trained fighting men. The tide has turned! The free men of the world are marching together to Victory! I have full confidence in your courage and devotion to duty and skill in battle. We will accept nothing less than full Victory! Good luck! And let us beseech the blessing of Almighty God upon this great and noble undertaking.
SIGNED: Dwight D. Eisenhower

Note. D-day statement to soldiers, sailors, and airmen of the Allied Expeditionary Force, 6/44, Collection DDE-EPRE: Eisenhower, Dwight D: Papers, Pre-Presidential, 1916-1952; Dwight D. Eisenhower Library; National Archives and Records Administration.

Watch Javier Vaca talking about planning a close reading at www.reading.org/ch2_planning or scan the QR code.

Ask Students to "Read With a Pencil"

After introducing the two pieces to her students to set the context, Ms. West asked them to read both independently. Importantly, she did not draw their attention to the dates or tell them about how they revealed Eisenhower's internal conflict. (Note: The original handwritten "In Case of Failure" memo is erroneously dated July 5 rather than June 5. Eisenhower later attributed this to "carelessness." We'll assume he had a lot on his mind that day.)

"It's important that they see the struggle leaders must confront, especially in having to keep these struggles fairly private," Ms. West said. Instead, she asked students to annotate the text, or as she puts it, "to read with a pencil," reminding them to circle words or phrases that are confusing, and to underline those that are powerful. (For more information on annotating text, please see the next chapter.) For the next several minutes, her students read silently and marked the text. Ms. West also had two students with disabilities that make it difficult for them to read the text independently; they listened to a podcast version of the two readings she made for them and followed along with the texts.

Remind Students to Note Confusions

As part of their interaction with the text, students should mark areas of confusion, typically by circling words or phrases that they are unsure of, and writing questions in the margin. Teachers should mark their own copies of the text to identify patterns of confusion for students, a great formative assessment practice.

Discuss the Text

Turning her attention to the class, Ms. West invited discussion. Knowing that it is often richer when students have an opportunity to first talk with peers in small groups, she said, "I'd like for you to talk about your initial impressions of these two readings with your table groups." As they talked, she visited several groups to listen to conversations, and then called the class back together. "So let's talk about this," she says. After each table shared summaries of its conversations, she transitioned to text-dependent questions to cause students to analyze the messages more closely.

Ask Text-Dependent Questions

The teacher seeded the discussion with text-dependent questions to encourage students to consider what the texts say, how they are structured and, most important, how they work together to tell us about the man who wrote them. She prepared the following questions and possible answers in advance so she could steer their attention as needed to evidence in the text. "I've got them understanding that they need to be able to support their assertions with evidence," she said. "But unless I know where that evidence is, it's really difficult for me to be able to teach toward the underlying patterns in the text."

Grounding Students in Foundational Understanding

- Reading 1: *Who is Eisenhower addressing?* (Allied troops) *What was the goal of the invasion?* (the destruction of the German war machine, the elimination of Nazi tyranny, and security for ourselves)
- Reading 2: *What event does Eisenhower describe?* (withdrawal of the troops) *Who does he fault?* (himself)

Examining Craft and Structure

- Reading 1: *What words and phrases does Eisenhower use to evoke religious images and ideology?* (Great Crusade, prayers, devotion, beseech the blessing of Almighty God) *What words and phrases does he use to inspire the troops as a righteous mission?* (liberty-loving people, free men of the world, great and noble undertaking)

- Reading 2: *Does Eisenhower use similar words and phrases in this message?* (Only one—Bravery and devotion to duty)

- Reading 1: *Eisenhower's message to the troops acknowledges the difficulty of the mission but assures them that they will be triumphant. In what ways does he accomplish this?* (He describes the fierceness of the enemy, the defeats and setbacks earlier in the war. But he also reminds them that there have been many victories since then. In addition, he reminds them of the support at home and in the collective strength of a multinational response. He also tells them of their skill, bravery, and training.) *Why is it essential that the general of the Allied Forces acknowledges both?* (If he doesn't, the troops might feel that he is not realistic, and does not understand the complexity of the invasion, and result in undermining their confidence in their leader. Their confidence in him and his judgment is essential to completing a successful mission.)

- Reading 2: *Eisenhower's tone is very different in the second message. What is the tone?* (His tone is terse and gets to the point. He doesn't blame anyone and places all fault on himself, even though many others were involved.) *Why is this an appropriate tone for a defeat?* (As a military general, it is important for him to demonstrate his leadership in defeat as well as in victory. Anyone can be triumphant; fewer are able to face defeat publicly in order to maintain his respect for his troops, demonstrate courage, and accept blame.)

The previous questions required students to shift their focus from one reading to the other. With these last questions, Ms. West wanted students to compare and contrast both documents in order to draw conclusions about the man who wrote them and the circumstances that prompted both.

Integrating Ideas Within and Across Documents

- Questions for both readings: *General Eisenhower wrote both of these messages within hours of one another. What conclusions do you draw about a man who must entertain two very different beliefs simultaneously?* (His leadership abilities were extraordinary in being able to exhort his troops before battle, while understanding the very real possibility that it might result in an awful defeat. It is likely that his pragmatic assessment of both possible outcomes is reflective of the care he had for his troops, as well as the great responsibility he carried on his shoulders. At the same time, it was necessary for him to be tough-minded and decisive. These traits are essential for military command.)

After this close reading of the two documents and discussion of these questions, Ms. West's students are ready to write. In the remaining time in the period, her students use evidence from both of these documents to address the following question:

The U.S. Army (Headquarters of the Department of the Army, 2007) lists 12 responsibilities of every military leader. Among them are the following:

- Ensure the physical, moral, personal, and professional wellbeing of subordinates.
- Effectively communicate vision, purpose, and direction.
- Build discipline while inspiring motivation, confidence, enthusiasm, and trust in subordinates.
- Anticipate and manage change and be able to act quickly and decisively under pressure.
- Treat subordinates with dignity, respect, fairness, and consistency.

In what ways do these two messages demonstrate General Eisenhower's commitment to his responsibilities? Be sure to use evidence from both texts to support your claims.

"As a U.S. history teacher, it's important that I use primary source documents so that students can witness history unfolding. Sometimes they view this only as being about events in the past, without fully appreciating the complexities of the moment," she said. "I hope that these experiences with close readings of text allow them to place themselves in the context of the times to more fully appreciate the uncertainty of the moment."

Text-Dependent Questions Focus on Evidence

Ms. West developed robust text-dependent questions to frame the discussion with her U.S. history students. Generally speaking, text-dependent questions require that evidence come from text, not information from outside sources. This does not mean that they are simply recall questions. Although initial text-dependent questions focus on the factual information found in the text, the questions should extend and deepen students' understanding by necessitating the use of critical thinking skills.

The CCSS have generated renewed interest in the types of questions students are asked related to the readings they do. This is due, in part, to the fact that students can answer many of the questions that teachers ask without ever reading the text, or by only giving it cursory attention. These text-*independent* questions are often interesting and generate a lot of discussion, but they do not ensure that students understand what they have read or that they can take issue with the author's perspective. Instead, they encourage students to make connections with their personal life and move further and further away from what the author offered. This is not to say that students should be prevented from linking their lives and knowledge to texts. In fact, Rosenblatt and many other theorists would argue that reading is transactional and transformative. However, a transaction implies that there are two parties, in this case a text and a reader. The quality of these connections is severely limited when the reader has only skimmed over the surface of a reading. In other words, a superficial understanding of a text is unlikely to provoke much in the way of meaningful connections across texts and experiences.

A key element of text-dependent questions is that they should direct students back into the text to locate evidence. By this, we mean not only that students name a sentence or paragraph where the information is found, but that they are able to do so in support of their analysis of evidence within and across texts. Examine the progression of textual evidence skills in Reading Standard 1 from grades 4–12 in English language arts, history, science, and technical subjects (see Table 2.2).

Table 2.2 Progression of Standards for Citing Textual Evidence

Reading: Key Ideas and Details for Literary and Informational Texts	
CCR Anchor Standard 1: Read closely to determine what the text says explicitly and to make logical inferences from it; cite specific textual evidence when writing or speaking to support conclusions drawn from the text.	
Grade	Grade-Specific Standard
Grade 6	Cite textual evidence to support analysis of what the text says explicitly as well as inferences drawn from the text.
Grade 7	Cite several pieces of textual evidence to support analysis of what the text says explicitly as well as inferences drawn from the text.
Grade 8	Cite the textual evidence that most strongly supports an analysis of what the text says explicitly as well as inferences drawn from the text.
Grades 9–10	Cite strong and thorough textual evidence to support analysis of what the text says explicitly as well as inferences drawn from the text.
Grades 11–12	Cite strong and thorough textual evidence to support analysis of what the text says explicitly as well as inferences drawn from the text, including determining where the text leaves matters uncertain.

Reading in History/Social Studies: Key Ideas and Details	
CCR Anchor Standard 1: Read closely to determine what the text says explicitly and to make logical inferences from it; cite specific textual evidence when writing or speaking to support conclusions drawn from the text.	
Grade	Grade-Band Standard
Grades 6–8	Cite specific textual evidence to support analysis of primary and secondary sources.
Grades 9–10	Cite specific textual evidence to support analysis of primary and secondary sources, attending to such features as the date and origin of the information.
Grades 11–12	Cite specific textual evidence to support analysis of primary and secondary sources, connecting insights gained from specific details to an understanding of the text as a whole.

Reading in Science and Technical Subjects: Key Ideas and Details	
CCR Anchor Standard 1: Read closely to determine what the text says explicitly and to make logical inferences from it; cite specific textual evidence when writing or speaking to support conclusions drawn from the text.	
Grade	Grade-Band Standard
Grades 6–8	Cite specific textual evidence to support analysis of science and technical texts.
Grades 9–10	Cite specific textual evidence to support analysis of science and technical texts, attending to the precise details of explanations or descriptions.
Grades 11–12	Cite specific textual evidence to support analysis of science and technical texts, attending to important distinctions the author makes and to any gaps or inconsistencies in the account.

You'll notice that in English, students move from citing several pieces of evidence in support of analysis, to being able to do so when the information is more ambiguous. In history, science, and technical subjects, the nature of the text itself changes: primary and secondary source documents in history; science and technical documents in the other disciplines. Moreover, students in history are challenged to look across documents, and those in science and the technical subjects progress from locating precise details to analyzing for gaps in information. Ms. West's U.S. history close reading was developed to encourage her students to analyze two documents.

Another detail that is easily overlooked in this progression has to do with the College and Career Readiness (CCR) Anchor Standards. Although it is located in the Reading domain, the CCR Anchor Standard clearly situates the practice of citing textual evidence across discussion and writing. The practice of close reading offers students guided instruction using reading, discussion, and writing.

Using the Standards to Develop Text-Dependent Questions

The CCR Anchor Standards for reading and literacy in the disciplines collectively describe what students should be able to do with complex texts by the time they graduate from high school. We have profiled Standard 1 (read closely to cite textual evidence) and Standard 10 (complex texts). Together these serve as bookends for Reading Standards 2–9. What occurs in between these bookends collectively describes the critical thinking that occurs when a reader deeply comprehends (see Table 2.3). These standards can also help us to develop a sequence of text-dependent questions that lead students down the three cognitive paths (e.g., Kurland, 1994; Shanahan, 2013): *What does the text say? How does the text work? What does the text mean?* Standards 2–9 are clustered into three groups: Key Ideas and Details, Craft and Structure, and Integration of Knowledge and Ideas. Close inspection reveals that the emphasis is on critical reading, interpretation, and evaluation, and not on simple recitations of facts. We will use a sixth-grade science teacher's selected reading passage about volcano hot spots to illustrate how each standard can play a role in the close reading and extended discussion of an informational text.

Table 2.3 College and Career Readiness Anchor Standards for Reading in ELA, History, Science, and Technical Subjects

Key Ideas and Details
1. Read closely to determine what the text says explicitly and to make logical inferences from it; cite specific textual evidence when writing or speaking to support conclusions drawn from the text. 2. Determine central ideas or themes of a text and analyze their development; summarize the key supporting details and ideas. 3. Analyze how and why individuals, events, and ideas develop and interact over the course of a text.
Craft and Structure
4. Interpret words and phrases as they are used in a text, including determining technical, connotative, and figurative meanings, and analyze how specific word choices shape meaning or tone. 5. Analyze the structure of texts, including how specific sentences, paragraphs, and larger portions of the text (e.g., a section, chapter, scene, or stanza) relate to each other and the whole. 6. Assess how point of view or purpose shapes the content and style of a text.
Integration of Knowledge and Ideas
7. Integrate and evaluate content presented in diverse formats and media, including visually and quantitatively, as well as in words. 8. Delineate and evaluate the argument and specific claims in a text, including the validity of the reasoning as well as the relevance and sufficiency of the evidence. 9. Analyze how two or more texts address similar themes or topics in order to build knowledge or to compare the approaches the authors take.
Range of Reading and Level of Text Complexity
10. Read and comprehend complex literary and informational texts independently and proficiently.

Key Ideas and Details

The first phrase in Standard 2 is "determining central ideas or themes," but it doesn't stop at identification. Students are to connect these elements in order to analyze how they are developed over the length of the piece and use them for the purpose of supporting summarization. Sixth-grade science teacher Bart Eggert selected a page from this science textbook for a close reading. "The [textbook] is great because it's visually powerful, but students tend to look at the sizzle and not evaluate the scientific principles that underpin a diagram. This is one of them," he said. He selected a full-page scientific illustration and accompanying text on intraplate volcanoes that form in the center, rather than on the boundaries of tectonic plates.

"They've been learning that lots of volcanoes occur in places where plates collide, but they don't realize that these 'hot spots' happen in lots of other places on Earth." Mr. Eggert explains that the key idea of this text is that volcanoes occur within plates and that the causation differs from boundary plate volcanoes. "I have to ask them questions that get them noticing that there's information in the text about mantle plumes that form between the mantle and core."

Standard 3 requires students to analyze how these key ideas and details unfold across the text. Mr. Eggert said,

> There are two elements in the illustration they need to notice: An arrow shows the direction of the tectonic plate's movement and the Hawaiian Islands featured next to it, along with text that says that "The oldest islands are farthest from the plume." Some of my questions will be to draw their attention to these elements so they can realize there's a conveyor belt effect going on here. The volcanoes keep forming and make a chain of islands. A lot of Earth Science deals with things that happen too fast or too slow to be seen.

He continued, "It's going to take some interpretation of information on their part to realize that the northwestern islands of Hawaii are five million years older than the southeastern end of the chain."

Craft and Structure

Standard 4 describes the importance of academic vocabulary in deep comprehension. "Lots of vocabulary, of course, in science," said Mr. Eggert, who continued,

> Of course there's terminology, but one detail they could easily overlook is that one portion of the text calls it a *mantle plume* and later a *magma plume*. I'll be asking them if the textbook writer got it wrong, or if there is a reason for the difference in terms. They'll need to study the illustration carefully to realize that the reason is because it refers to the relative location of the plume in the layers of the Earth. This should reinforce one of the key details: These volcanoes form between the mantle and core.

Standard 5 calls for students to consider the role of text organization both within and across the text. Increasingly, science texts include both written text and illustrations to convey complex concepts. "I think I'm going to start by making sure they are reading and analyzing all of the information on the page," Mr. Eggert said, who further stated,

> Sometimes they don't know where to put their eyes. Just on this one page there's the primary block of text, additional text that is positioned and numbered to represent elapsed time, and an inset map illustration of Hawaii. My first questions will be related to how they read this.

Standard 6 asks students to assess purpose or point of view as it relates to the content and style of the text. "This is my opportunity to really get them thinking about why the writer included all of these visual and textual elements," Mr. Eggert said, who continued,

> The illustration shows a cross-section of the Earth's crust, including the mantle and crust, but they aren't labeled as such. You have to read the primary text in order to infer that detail. There's a sentence in there that describes the movement of the plate over the plume, which is represented as arrows in the illustration. I'll be asking them questions about the decision to use words in some cases and visual elements in others to exemplify this phenomenon.

Integration of Knowledge and Ideas

Standard 7 challenges students to integrate content presented through diverse formats, and Mr. Eggert's choice is ideal. "This isn't applicable to everything we read, but scientific illustrations and visualizations are certainly a part of the materials we use in class." As an extension of this close reading, he plans on having his students view a short video that discusses geologic hotspots:

> After we view the video tomorrow, I am going to have them return to this reading and ask them to speculate as to why the older islands are smaller than the younger ones. It will give me a chance to see whether they are applying what they have previously learned about erosion.

Standard 8 requires students to evaluate arguments and claims, as well as whether the evidence is sufficient. Mr. Eggert said,

> Some scientific knowledge is speculative, and there's an important part of the passage I want them to discuss. I'll point this out to them, as it uses words such as *uncertain* and *probably*. I'll be asking them about other

sources we can consult to confirm this uncertainty, and we'll learn whether there are alternative proposals about the origin of hotspots.

Mr. Eggert plans to use the textbook passage and the video to address some of the issues Standard 9 raises:

> As a science person, I am all about consulting multiple sources to learn about phenomena. I want my students to understand that inquiry is the heart of science. In order for them to be scientifically literate, they need to develop this habit. Tomorrow, my text-dependent questions will invite comparison.

Mr. Eggert's analysis of Standards 2–9 suggests that he grounds his practice of question-driven discussion of science texts to develop students who think critically. "One of the biggest lessons I have had to learn is to remember not to say what I think [his students] can say." When asked to explain himself further, he said,

> I've spent a lot of years telling kids everything I know about science. It took me a long time to realize that unless I can get them talking about science, they're not going to remember much. I try to develop questions that get them thinking, rather than me just telling them what to think.

Text-Level Specificity

In order to address these learning purposes, the text-dependent questions we use should alternatively zoom in on details and zoom out to view the text as a whole. We guide our students' attention relative to text specificity, which is different from saying we are teaching strictly part-to-whole. This should not be seen as a rigid hierarchy or that the questions must be asked in any particular order. However, it is essential to understand that different types of knowledge are used when deeply understanding a text. The discussions generated through the use of text-dependent questions are intended to facilitate analysis at the micro and macro levels.

Text-Dependent Questions About Words and Phrases

Some text-dependent questions are about vocabulary words and phrases (Standard 4) as well as looking closely at shorter passages within the text in order (Standard 5). Questions at the word and phrase level can support students' initial understanding of the literal meaning of the text in the early phases of the lesson. Later on, these questions target the author's craft about word choice as it relates to style (Standard 6).

Text-Dependent Questions About Specific Sentences and Paragraphs

Attention to sentences means attention to syntax, "which gives the words power to relate to each other in a sequence, to create rhythms and emphasis, to carry meaning—of whatever kind—as well as glow individually in just the right place" (Tufte, 2006, p. 1). Text-dependent questions at the sentence level assist students in locating key details (Standard 2) and the purpose and point of view of the piece (Standard 6); sequencing the development of characters, events, and ideas (Standard 3); and delineating arguments (Standard 8). This last intent is crucial for students who are not adept at linking arguments with reasoning, and questions that zoom in at the sentence and paragraph levels can assist them in parsing the text.

Text-Dependent Questions About Longer Passages

Longer passages and sections of a text provide readers with the opportunity to analyze how a writer shapes content (Standard 6) and employs text types (Standard 5). Central themes and ideas begin to emerge at this level (Standard 2).

Text-Dependent Questions About the Piece as a Whole

Once again, the structure of the text reveals how the plot is developed or the information is presented (Standard 5). In addition, readers begin to evaluate the text itself (Standard 7) and link central ideas to key details (Standard 2). As well, they can analyze how characters or ideas evolved over the course of the entire text (Standard 3). For texts that contain significant elements of formal argumentation, students evaluate the validity of the argument and the robustness of the evidence used by the writer (Standard 8).

Text-Dependent Questions Across Texts and Platforms

In some cases, close readings encompass two or more documents. At other times, information may be enhanced through the use of complex diagrams, multimedia, or graphics. Students must integrate information from multiple sources and determine where the intersections lie between them, as well as when they may contradict (Standard 7). Ms. West's examination of two documents written by the same man on the same day focused on the similarities and differences between the two.

Using Text-Dependent Questions in Middle School English

There are questions that focus on parts of texts, and there are questions that focus on whole texts. As we have noted, these types of questions have one thing in common: They require that readers have read and understood the text. Ideally, some text-dependent questions that students are asked will require that they return to the text and reread to find evidence. It is also important to note that simply asking text-dependent questions will not ensure that students suddenly develop the ability to read and understand complex texts. Students still need to be taught how to read deeply and how to respond with evidence from the text.

Watch Augusto Ejanda talking about creating questions at www.reading.org/ ch2_creating or scan the QR code.

For now, we'll focus on the types of questions that are useful in ensuring students have read the text. For each type of question, we'll provide examples of questions that Bryan Cale asked of his eighth graders as they studied "Jabberwocky" by Lewis Carroll (1872/1999). The text of the poem appears in Figure 2.3.

What Is This Text About?

These questions ensure that students grasp the overall view of the text. Often they are global questions, but questions that require that students demonstrate an understanding of what the author really said. Depending on the type of text, these questions may probe the sequence of information presented, the story arc, the main claim and evidence presented, or the gist of a given passage.

"In 'Jabberwocky,'" Mr. Cale asked, "what is the progress of the hero?" As students worked in their triads to construct the story arc, Mr. Cale

Figure 2.3 "Jabberwocky" by Lewis Carroll

`Twas brillig, and the slithy toves
Did gyre and gimble in the wabe:
All mimsy were the borogoves,
And the mome raths outgrabe.
"Beware the Jabberwock, my son!
The jaws that bite, the claws that catch!
Beware the Jubjub bird, and shun
The frumious Bandersnatch!"
He took his vorpal sword in hand:
Long time the manxome foe he sought—
So rested he by the Tumtum tree,
And stood awhile in thought.
And, as in uffish thought he stood,
The Jabberwock, with eyes of flame,
Came whiffling through the tulgey wood,
And burbled as it came!
One, two! One, two! And through and through
The vorpal blade went snicker-snack!
He left it dead, and with its head
He went galumphing back.
"And, has thou slain the Jabberwock?
Come to my arms, my beamish boy!
O frabjous day! Callooh! Callay!"
He chortled in his joy.
`Twas brillig, and the slithy toves
Did gyre and gimble in the wabe;
All mimsy were the borogoves,
And the mome raths outgrabe.

Note. From *Through the Looking-Glass and What Alice Found There*, by L. Carroll 1872/1999.

moved from group to group, checking their understanding. As members of each group returned to the text for discussion, they charted their understanding with variations of the fact that the hero had a warning, set off to deal with the monster, experienced conquest, and returned triumphantly.

In What Ways Does the Structure Help Us Understand the Text?

In developing questions about text structure, Mr. Cale wanted to focus on the real words and the structure of the poem, starting with the questions, "What type of poem is this? Knowing the structure, what do we expect?"

For the first question, every group identified the poem as a ballad, in which the identical first and last four lines enclose five stanzas. They also discussed the idea that this would have been sung or chanted aloud and that this specific type, heroic, should chart the progress of the hero.

What Are the Key Details That Help Us Unlock the Meaning?

These text-dependent questions require that readers pay attention to the details. As such, they are able to respond to questions that ask *who, what, when, where, why, how much,* or *how many.* They also must search for nuances in meaning, determine importance of ideas, and find supporting details for the main ideas.

For "Jabberwocky," Mr. Cale asked questions to ensure that students were making sense of the nonsense words as well as the fact that the Jabberwock was slain. "What were the slithy toves doing in the wabe?" The students quickly answered, "gyre and gimble." "But what does that mean?" Mr. Cale asked. "How would you describe the condition of the borogoves?" He let the students struggle a bit longer with the text before sharing some of the information that Lewis Carroll provided at the time of publication, namely that *gyre* in the second line is "to scratch" and *gimble* is defined as "to bore holes." "Does that help?" he asked, and they nodded. Then he turned his attention to the main idea, asking, "Who killed the Jabberwock?" The students read, and reread the poem, certain that they would find the answer. Finally, one group said, "It's got to be anonymous. There are all kinds of words we don't know, but none of the stanzas tell us who the boy is. That detail isn't there."

How Do Words and Phrases Impact the Meaning?

These text-dependent questions focus on the specific words and phrases the author uses. This requires that the reader bridge literal and inferential meanings, noting both denotation (literal or primary word meanings) and connotation (the idea or feeling that a word invokes) as well as the shades of meaning elicited by the word choice. For example, an author might use the word *walk, stroll, amble, saunter, meander,* or *wander.* The shades of meaning are different, and readers should take note of these choices. Further, readers should notice figurative language and how the organization of the text contributes to meaning.

Who Is the Author, and What Is the Point of View?

Although often not specifically stated, there is a purpose for each text. Sometimes, the genre or the text type helps the reader understand the author's purpose. Was the specific text written to convey an experience, inform, or persuade? Other times, the way in which the author constructs the text—the point of view—helps readers determine the purpose. First-person texts tell the reader one thing while third-person limited versus omniscient tell the reader something else. Further, texts are told from a specific vantage point and readers want to know, whose story is *not* represented? Mr. Cale asked his students about the author's purpose, including the choice of narrator. As students discussed this, he noted their understanding of the difference between first person and third person and the influence that point of view has on understanding and perspective.

What Are Our Interpretations of This Text?

Inferences are more than guesses or simply telling students to "read between the lines." Readers should know how to probe each argument in persuasive text, each idea in informational text, and each key detail in literary text and to observe how these build to a whole. Text-dependent questions should allow students to consider the information that is provided and then make informed interpretations.

When Mr. Cale moved to these questions, he started with a fairly obvious one. "How did the narrator know the Jabberwock was dead, not the Jubjub bird or Bandersnatch?" The conversation was lively and included a discussion about bringing back the head of the Jabberwock. Several students noted that this was common in history, to keep the head to show that the enemy was really dead. He then asked, "What can we infer about the Jabberwock, given the text and his name?" As the students discussed this with their groups, most believed that it was a monster, citing evidence that it has "jaws that bite and claws that catch." Others said that the name was important, "jabber is to talk a lot, my mom says that all of the time, so I think that it could be one of those birds that copies what people say, but a mean one." Mr. Cale noted the confusion that his students had about inferencing and decided to model his thinking aloud for students to provide them with additional practice in this area.

What Are Our Informed Judgments About This Text?

The final category of text-dependent questions often contains the questions that teachers like to ask best because these usually generate a lot of discussion. When they follow a discussion built on text-dependent questions, they work well for this purpose. If they are used in place of text-dependent questions, the risk is that students will answer and not need to read the text. As such, teachers can unintentionally telegraph a message to students suggesting that reading and understanding are not necessary. When these questions are used, they can analyze claims, evidence, and counterclaims. They can also encourage students to consider logic and rhetoric, such as ethos, logos, and pathos.

Mr. Cale offered students the choice between two questions for their group to consider. They were to summarize their responses in writing. He reminded them that they had to use evidence from the text in their discussions about their answers. These were the options:

1. According to the poem, how should we construct our notions of good and evil?
2. Why is the hero of the poem—the ultimate good guy who slays the Jabberwock—anonymous?

The students knew a great deal about this poem; they understood it fairly well because of the questions they were asked and the interactions they had with their peers and their teachers. One group summarized their response as follows:

> There is a lot of evil in the world. The parent tells his son to beware. But the son is good and wants to take care of the problem. He leaves on a journey to fight the evil beings—Jabberwock, Jubjub bird, and Bandersnatch—taking his sword. In this poem, good won over bad but there is still more evil in the world because the Jubjub bird and Bandersnatch are still alive.

It's More Than Recall

Text-dependent questions do not have to focus exclusively on recall and recitation of information. Instead, they can be invitations for students to think deeply about a text and compare it with their own perspectives and experiences. Text-dependent questions do require that students provide evidence from the text and encourage students to reread the text. As we have noted, not all texts require this level of investigation. Sometimes, students read for pleasure and entertainment. Other times, readers want or need to understand the text at a much deeper level. In those cases, text-dependent questions can guide students' thinking and build habits that they can apply widely.

Conclusion

The factors that make a text complex include quantitative and qualitative measures such as content, cohesion, and organization. In turn, both the reader and the task must be considered in making these determinations. Importantly, text differs across disciplines, and many students are not equipped to engage in deep understanding of the readings that define a content area. The practice of close reading invites students to read repeatedly, and is guided by discussion of text-dependent questions. When practices such as close reading are consistently implemented across content areas, students become better equipped to handle more difficult texts.

CHAPTER 3

Preparing for Discussion and Writing: Annotation, Sourcing, and Avoiding Plagiarism

Watch Doug introduce the chapter at www.reading.org/ch3_intro or scan the QR code.

Both of us teach at a university, and we often encounter graduates from our high school on campus. Most of them are doing well, and we enjoy hearing them talk about their college classes. But many have remarked on the comparative lack of support for their reading. "They just assign us all these readings, like a couple hundred pages a week," Amir told us. "We're expected to know the content, but no one ever has us read and discuss in class. Makes me appreciate what we used to do in high school," he said.

It's nice to hear that some students recognize the value, however belatedly, of the close readings and text-based discussions in their high school classes. We asked Amir how he was faring, and he reported that he was doing well despite a heavy course load. "I know how to talk back to a text," he told us. "I read with my pencil, just like we were taught. Not all my friends know how to do that."

In this chapter, we address the multifaceted issue of preparing for discussions and writing. These are essential skills for achieving the goals set forth by the CCSS, notably:

- Prepare for and participate effectively in a range of conversations (SL.CCR.1)
- Present information, findings, and supporting evidence such that listeners can follow the line of reading and organization (SL.CCR.4)
- Develop and strengthen writing as needed by planning (W.CCR.5)
- Gather relevant information from multiple print and digital sources... while avoiding plagiarism (W.CCR.8)

- Draw evidence from literary or informational texts to support analysis, reflection, and research (W.CCR.9)

This process begins with annotation or, as Amir said, "reading with a pencil." Initially, it serves the function of promoting active reading and lives on after readers return to texts to find evidence. As students move from reading to researching, they use their annotations for sourcing evidence and to develop an outline for the essay or report. In the last part of the chapter, we turn our attention to preventing plagiarism.

Teaching Students to Read With a Pencil

The notes in a book can reveal much about the reader. Edgar Allan Poe (1844/1988), himself an unapologetic penciler, wrote "in the marginalia, too, we talk only to ourselves; we therefore talk freshly—boldly— originally—with abandonment—without conceit" (p. 483). The practice of making notes to oneself during a reading was for centuries a widespread practice, but it fell out of favor in the 20th century as public libraries became common. To write in a book was thought to sully it somehow. To be sure, writing in a text that doesn't belong to you isn't looked upon kindly. But in the process of protecting the public books, we forgot about the gains to be had from writing in one that belongs to us alone.

In their seminal text *How to Read a Book*, Adler and Van Doren (1940/1972) laid out a case for engaging in repeated readings with accompanying annotation:

> Why is marking a book indispensable to reading it? First, it keeps you awake—not merely conscious, but wide awake. Second, reading, if active, is thinking, and thinking tends to express itself in words, spoken or written. The person who says he knows what he thinks but cannot express it usually does not know what he thinks. Third, writing your reactions down helps you remember the thoughts of the author. (p. 49)

They go on to describe the most common annotation marks:

- *Underlining* for major points.
- *Vertical lines in the margin* to denote longer statements that are too long to be underlined.

- *Star, asterisk, or other doodad in the margin* to be used sparingly to emphasize the ten or dozen most important statements. You may want to fold a corner of each page where you make such a mark or place a slip of paper between the pages.

- *Numbers in the margin* to indicate a sequence of points made by the author in development of an argument.

- *Numbers of other pages in the margin* to indicate where else in the book the author makes the same points.

- *Circling of key words or phrases* to serve much the same function as underlining.

- *Writing in the margin, or at the top or bottom of the page* to record questions (and perhaps answers) which a passage raises in your mind. (pp. 49–50)

Watch Angie Holbrook talking about teaching annotation at www.reading.org/ ch3_annotation or scan the QR code.

The authors advocated for the use of annotations for two important reasons: First, because the act of marking a text strengthens ownership in terms of property as well as intellect. Second, because annotation changes the reading from a lecture to a conversation between you and the author as you express "your differences or agreements...[i]t is the highest respect you can pay him." (p. 49).

When Doug read this passage several years ago, he had his own moment of realization. As a financially challenged college student, he had routinely purchased used textbooks, but was choosy about his final selection. No annotations? He'd put it back on the pile because the previous owner hadn't read it. Too much highlighting? That person couldn't tell the difference between what was important and what wasn't. The "just right" used textbooks contained thoughtful annotations. His moment of realization was in understanding that the carefully annotated ones allowed him to converse with two people: the author and a previous reader.

Nancy recalls shopping at the grocery store just before a major holiday when the store was at its busiest. She noticed a shopping list in the bottom of the cart she found. On it were all the ingredients of a traditional meal, some crossed off, as well as a few errands to be run. But what made it memorable was the message written at the bottom in capital letters: "DON'T LOSE LIST!" Too late.

We write things down to remember them. We make lists and use them to remind us what needs to be done. But if we don't return to them, their usefulness is reduced. We require students to annotate during reading because it promotes active reading and gives them a tool for monitoring their comprehension. But if we don't provide them with reasons to return to their annotations, we limit the potential of this tool. What they have on the pages in front of them is a visual record of their thinking—ideally of use in discussions and as a means for developing a written response.

Whether constructed independently or collaboratively, annotations can be used as an early form of composition. Encourage students to use the annotations they made while reading a text to drive the written summary, especially for longer or more complex readings. Remind students that argumentative essays are extended dialogue with and about one or more pieces of text and that their annotations help guide this flow of information. Make sure students see the usefulness in their annotations as a means for later developing a more formal written piece. The questions or points of agreement and disagreement that they initially annotate in the margins can become the main thesis of their essays.

Annotation in High School English

Eleventh-grade English teacher Marcus Boulanger asks his students to annotate text as they read short stories. "With the Common Core [State Standards] asking us to up the text complexity, I realized that students needed lots more experience with how to do this," he said. Many of his students are good readers, but they have what Mr. Boulanger calls a "naïve understanding" of their ability to hold extensive amounts of information in their minds. "Some of them think that reading is reading, whether it's a novel you're reading at the beach or a scientific paper about an experiment," he said.

Mr. Boulanger introduced his students to a method of annotation similar to the one described by Adler and Van Doren at the beginning of the school year, and his students now use this method when engaged in close readings. After the class had read the short story "Sonny's Blues" (Baldwin, 1965) for the first time, students returned to the reading, this time examining it more closely for themes. Mr. Boulanger had created a copy of the text with a column for annotated notes on the left side of the pages so that students could write on the text. At his direction, they combed the reading to find examples of Baldwin's use of darkness and light as a way to contrast the relationship between the two brothers. The students then discussed this imagery in their table groups:

Khadijah: I underlined right here where he said that, "the bright sun deadened his dark brown damp skin" because I could imagine how sickly Sonny must have looked in the outside light.

Paco: That's good, yeah, you're right. I wrote a note to myself about him bein' in the club, and there were jazz musicians. I was thinking 'bout there being a piano there, and the keys are black and white…

Elisa: And you play different notes, like some are sharp and some are flat.

Khadijah: Sounds like those piano lessons finally paid off for you.

Elisa: [laughs] Yeah, but it's true. I marked this part where the narrator is talking about when the old folks are all together and it's just starting to get dark…

Paco: Yeah, and the kid is scared that things will change, and then it says… Wait, I circled it right here…

Elisa: I got it. "And when the light fills the room, the child is filled with darkness. He knows that every time this happens, he's moved just a little closer to the darkness outside."

Khadijah: It's like that poem we read, about "Nothing gold can stay." You're a little kid, but you're growing up, and you know that feeling safe and protected is going to go away.

By annotating texts, whether informational, persuasive, or narrative, students learn to slow down their reading to mine the depths of the concepts, arguments, and metaphors used by the writer. While this practice isn't necessary, or even desirable, for everything students read, it is important when the information in the text requires close inspection to unlock its meaning. It is also a practical tool for students to use to support their discussion of texts with peers.

Using Annotation to Support Content Instruction

Well-designed discussions that draw on student annotations reinforce the practice of annotating. Annotations can drive instruction when teachers review the annotations and determine what students understand, both in terms of content and process. And annotations provide students with the notes they need to furnish evidence that supports their thinking. It would be a mistake to expect that students' annotations are always going to be correct or that their reasoning will be sound. But discussions that consistently return students back to the original texts and to the text they have created (i.e., their annotations) are effective for shaping their thinking. Remember when we said, "Read with a pencil?" That's because we want students to revise and update their annotations throughout the discussion process. Once again, this practice gives them a means for monitoring their understanding. As an example, we have included a student's annotation of the poem "In Flanders Fields" (McCrae, 1915) after her first reading (see Figure 3.1). It's obvious that this student has a lot of questions about the text and that she has some understanding of what the author is trying to say. When asked to summarize her understanding of the text, Yareli wrote, "I believe the message is to tell soldiers to go and win the battle, 'To you from falling hands we throw the torch.' It also says that they should bring glory to the fallen soldiers or else they won't rest, when the text says, 'We shall not sleep.'"

The students in Joanna Schaefer's world history class are learning about Russia in the 1920s. At this point in the semester, the students have learned about the Russian Revolution and the removal and murder of the Romanov family. They understand the difference between economic systems (e.g., socialism and capitalism) and government structures (e.g., monarchy, democracy, communism). As part of their class, they regularly encounter complex texts. They are also practiced at productive group work and know that their teacher models her thinking for them.

Watch Joanna Schaefer talking about her history lesson at www.reading.org/ch3_lesson or scan the QR code.

One of the texts they read is *Industrialization of the Country, 1928* by Joseph Stalin (see Figure 3.2). Ms. Schaefer asks her students to read the text independently, annotating key points and big ideas. She then invites

Figure 3.1 Sample Student Annotation

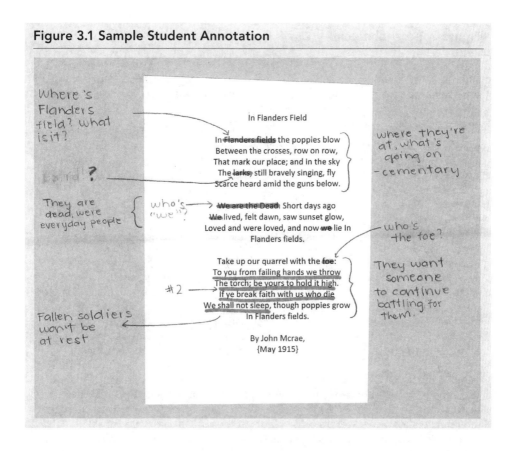

Where's Flanders field? what is it?

land ?

They are dead, were everyday people

Fallen soldiers won't be at rest

In Flanders Field

In Flanders fields the poppies blow
Between the crosses, row on row,
That mark our place; and in the sky
The larks still bravely singing, fly
Scarce heard amid the guns below.

who's "we"?

We are the Dead. Short days ago
We lived, felt dawn, saw sunset glow,
Loved and were loved, and now we lie In
Flanders fields.

#2

Take up our quarrel with the foe:
To you from failing hands we throw
The torch; be yours to hold it high.
If ye break faith with us who die
We shall not sleep, though poppies grow
In Flanders fields.

By John Mcrae,
{May 1915}

where they're at, what's going on
- cementary

who's the foe?

They want someone to continue battling for them.

her students to talk with a partner about the purpose of the text by asking them, "What was Stalin trying to accomplish in this speech? Be sure to use your annotations to provide your evidence." The answers varied but were centered on the idea that Stalin wanted to motive his people to focus on industry. Several groups noted that the motivation was to compete with other countries. As Marco said, "I think Stalin was so focused on Germany because of World War I. Germany declared war on Russia and a lot of Russian people died."

Concerned that her students could drift too far away from the text before they fully understood it, she asked them to look closely at the text and determine "in which areas is the Soviet Union behind, at least according to Stalin?" She reminds them to record their information as annotations so they could use their notes when they wrote their reports.

Figure 3.2 Joseph Stalin (1879–1953): *Industrialization of the Country, 1928*

Between 1928 and 1933, Stalin inaugurated the First and Second Five-Year Plans to achieve his goal of rapid industrialization. In many respects he was successful—by 1939 the USSR was behind only the United States and Germany in industrial output. The human costs, however, were enormous.

The question of a fast rate of development of industry would not face us so acutely as it does now if we had such a highly developed industry and such a highly developed technology as Germany, Say, and if the relative importance of industry in the entire national economy were as high in our country as it is in Germany, for example. If that were the case, we could develop our industry at a slower rate without fearing to fall behind the capitalist countries and knowing that we could outstrip them at one stroke. But then we should not be so seriously backward technically and economically as we are now. The whole point is that we are behind Germany in this respect and are still far from having overtaken her technically and economically.

The question of a fast rate of development of industry would not face us so acutely if we were not the only country but one of the countries of the dictatorship of the proletariat, if there were a proletarian dictatorship not only in our country but in other, more advanced countries as well, Germany and France, say.

If that were the case, the capitalist encirclement could not be so serious a danger as it is now, the question of the economic independence of our country would naturally recede into the background, we could integrate ourselves into the system of more developed proletarian states, we could receive from them machines for making our industry and agriculture more productive, supplying them in turn with raw materials and foodstuffs, and we could, consequently, expand our industry at a slower rate. But you know very well that that is not yet the case and that we are still the only country of the proletarian dictatorship and are surrounded by capitalist countries, many of which are far in advance of us technically and economically.

Internal conditions. But besides the external conditions, there are also internal conditions which dictate a fast rate of development of our industry as the main foundation of our entire national economy. I am referring to the extreme backwardness of our agriculture, of its technical and cultural level. I am referring to the existence in our country of an overwhelming preponderance of small commodity producers, with their scattered and utterly backward production, compared with which our large-scale socialist industry is like an island in the midst of the sea, an island whose base is expanding daily, but which is nevertheless an island in the midst of the sea.

External conditions. We have assumed power in a country whose technical equipment is terribly backward. Along with a few big industrial units more or less based upon modem technology, we have hundreds and thousands of mills and factories the technical equipment of which is beneath all criticism from the point of view of modem achievements. At the same time we have around us a number of capitalist countries whose industrial technique is far more developed and up-to-date than that of our country. Look at the capitalist countries and you will see that their

(continued)

Figure 3.2 Joseph Stalin (1879–1953): *Industrialization of the Country, 1928* **(continued)**

technology is not only advancing, but advancing by leaps and bounds, outstripping the old forms of industrial technique. And so we find that, on the one hand, we in our country have the most advanced system, the Soviet system, and the most advanced type of state power in the world, Soviet power, while, on the other hand, our industry, which should be the basis of socialism and of Soviet power, is extremely backward technically. Do you think that we can achieve the final victory of socialism in our country so long as this contradiction exists?

What has to be done to end this contradiction? To end it, we must overtake and outstrip the advanced technology of the developed capitalist countries. We have overtaken and outstripped the advanced capitalist countries in the sense of establishing a new political system, the Soviet system. That is good. But it is not enough. In order to secure the final victory of socialism in our country, we must also overtake and outstrip these countries technically and economically. Either we do this, or we shall be forced to the wall.

Note. From "Industrialization of the Country and the Right Deviation in the C.P.S.U., November 19,1928," in *Works*, Vol. 11, 1928–March 1929, pp. 257–58, 261–63, by J. Stalin, 1954, Moscow: Foreign Languages Publishing House.

"Don't just underline. I want you to write a statement, observation, or question you have about this." The groups searched the text and identified industry and technology and exchanged information about what they had written. Ms. Schaefer then asked, "Who is Stalin saying his country is behind? The obvious answer is Germany, but there is more to it. Take a look and talk with your group." As the students reread and discuss, they identify France, the other country explicitly named in the text.

Ms. Schaefer decides to model some of her thinking for her students because they have missed a key point in Stalin's speech. She says,

> I'm thinking about the line when Stalin says "outstrip them in one stroke" because he doesn't say *it*, meaning one country, he says *them*. I want to reread that section and see if I can figure out who Stalin is referring to. I know that he has a beef with Germany overall, but the word *them* is important. When I reread I noticed that he says "capitalist countries," and there are several of them. I think that Stalin is trying to tell his people that the world is leaving them behind, and that it's bigger than their problems with Germany because he says that they are "seriously backward," which is really offensive, or it would be to me if I heard this speech about my people. So I think he must be trying to tell people that their country is at risk when compared with a lot of other countries, not just Germany and France.

She continues,

> So now I want you to look at the annotation you just made about capitalist countries. Draw on what you know about the world at that time. Who else is Stalin referring to, even if they are unnamed? As you talk to each other, add this information to your annotation.

"It's like Voldemort in *Harry Potter*," said Myra. "You know, 'He who will not be named.' Who are the bogeymen for Stalin?" Stanley writes down *like Voldemort* on his annotated text, and adds, "The United States and Great Britain are the ones he's scared of the most."

Ms. Schaefer poses another question. "How does Stalin feel about 'capitalist countries'? And don't just say an answer. I want you to use evidence to justify your response." The students talk about envy, namely that "Stalin is really jealous of what the capitalist countries have and maybe a little fearful that they will be taken over by these countries." They noted, "He even says that 'we shall be forced to the wall,' which is how they put people in the firing squad to kill them." Once again, Ms. Schaefer reminds students to add information as needed to their annotations.

She then asks students to identify the goals that Stalin has. They talk about making industry more productive and providing food for the people. The students also discuss the idea the USSR is "surrounded by capitalist countries" and that Stalin seems afraid of that because they are more advanced technically and economically. One student, Annalisa, said, "I see a little fear in this because of his word choice *surrounded*. It's like he's looking to every border of his country and seeing places that are better off. It's really a call to action, I think." Marco adds, "He's talking about being an island. That's definitely a sign that he feels surrounded." Ms. Schaefer responds, "That's another great example. Be sure to add that as an example of his mindset if you haven't already."

As their close reading continues, Ms. Schaefer asks her students why Stalin believes that the people of USSR must support his five-year plan. She also asks students to identify the key ideas in this speech by asking, "What does Stalin want his people to do, specifically?" As students infer the connotations of *outstrip* and *overtake*, they develop an appreciation for the tension between the two countries.

The next question requires students to make connections between several texts and to apply their background knowledge. Ms. Schaefer asks, "If you were president of the United States at that time, or the leader of another capitalist country, and you heard this speech, what would you be thinking?" The students begin talking about being "on alert" and worrying that "they were going to steal our secrets and try to have better machines than us."

And her final question, "For whom was this speech written?" generated a great deal of discussion. Jeremy summarized his group's thinking by saying,

> Obviously, he was speaking to the people of the USSR. But he had to know that the leaders of other countries would hear or read his speech, so there are things he includes to put them on notice that the conflict is not over. The best evidence we have for this is his line, "Do you think that we can achieve the final victory of socialism in our country so long as this contradiction exists?" Stalin is saying that the final, final victory is not yet determined. Yes, they have an advanced "state power" but they have not yet had victory.

This text was complex, to be sure, and it took time and discussion for the students to understand it deeply. The teacher's repeated reminders to alter and add to their annotations were intended so that students could trace their evolution of thought and to capture insights in the moment that might otherwise fade quickly. Ms. Schaefer's students regularly engage in writing that requires them to return to primary source documents. Their revised annotations provide students with a record of the analysis developed collectively in class.

Using Collaborative Annotation

Collaborative annotation encourages students to work together as they read and discuss text. One way to accomplish this is by enlarging a passage on a poster and giving students highlighters and pencils to collectively annotate pages. (We ask students to use a pencil rather than a pen so they can easily change their notes as their thinking evolves.) Science teacher Charlie Larson uses collaborative annotation in advance of labs his middle school students will complete. "They get all the materials in front of them, and they want to go to town," he said. "The procedural information and the questions to promote scientific thinking are on the lab sheet, but they rush through it." Mr. Larson now has lab partners collaboratively annotate poster-sized lab sheets before they get to work.

Students read and mark the text together, using a protocol of Mr. Larson's own devising.

- Circle the verbs and write a synonym in the margin.
- Draw a slash and write the phrase "stop and observe" at each point in the lab where this will be necessary.
- Write questions about anything that is not clear to you and your partner so I can answer them.

"As they meet, I walk around and read their annotations," said Mr. Larson. "I get a quick measure of how well they understand what they will need to do." He instructs students to leave their collaboratively annotated lab sheets on the wall so they can consult them throughout the lesson:

> As I meet with each group I refer to their annotated lab sheet to see if they are doing what they said they would do. It's also made me get better at writing labs so that they are clear and worded in such a way that I am prompting their critical thinking, not just completing a procedure.

When students begin to write their lab report together, they return to their annotated version one more time. "It helps them to remember what they were thinking about before they performed the experiment, which makes it easier for them to reflect on their learning," said Mr. Larson.

Digital Collaborative Annotation

Keep in mind that collaborative annotations are easier than ever with digital tools. Beach (2012) describes these as a means for creating a "digital learning commons" because students can collectively assemble their annotations and provoke extended digital conversations. For example, most electronic book readers and tablets have an annotation feature that will amass the notes made by all using the feature. The Kindle book reader has a Public Notes feature that makes the notes available to anyone who has the text. A teacher can annotate an electronic text in advance, including questions and comments, for students to read. Diigo and Notability are popular tools for classroom use because they work on several popular platforms. Our students have also used Markup, which can be added to the toolbar of a web browser and used to annotate websites (Frey, Fisher, & Gonzalez, 2013).

Watch Alex Gonzalez talking about text annotation tools at www.reading.org/ch3_tools or scan the QR code.

Preparation Through Note-Taking

The purpose of annotating directly on a reading is to strengthen the transaction that occurs between a reader and the text. This is further enhanced when students have the opportunity to revise their annotations during discussion and through other collaborative arrangements. But there comes a time when students need to move from the print or digital page to the construction of prepared notes. The sources of information for notes include lectures and multimedia as well as written work. Notes are organized and contain more information than annotations typically do. Properly executed, they are short summaries of information that are used as building blocks for constructing presentations and writing. If annotations are a visual record of a running dialogue with a text, then notes are an organized synthesis of those conversations.

Developing Notes About Classroom Instruction

The act of transforming information learned during classroom instruction onto a page has a modest but positive effect on learning. According to a number of studies focused on the impact of encoding information, groups of students who took notes outperformed those who only listened or read, especially for students in grades 6–12 (Kobayashi, 2005). The overall length of the lecture also seems to have an impact this, ideally coming in 20-minute chunks. The real power of note-taking occurs when students have a chance to review what they wrote later, as it gives learners a critical first opportunity to synthesize information. Indeed, when initial note-taking is combined with review of notes, the impact on learning increases significantly (Hattie, 2009).

Ninth-grade geography teacher Wren Washington makes sure her students understand that the value of their notes lies in what they do with them. "When I first started teaching, I was all about giving kids points for having a complete notebook," she chuckled, and continued:

> I'd have notebook checks twice a quarter, and I'd see lots of really beautiful notes from some of my students. But I began to realize that there wasn't

much connection between who was getting the maximum number of points on their notebook checks, and who was doing well on the tests I was giving.

Her conversations with students helped her to understand that while many of them were putting their energy into making their notes, few ever looked back at them later. After doing some research on her own, she found a tool that proved to be useful for her students (Figure 3.3). This self-assessment of notes by Stahl, King, and Henk (1991) draws on the research on metacognitive awareness and requires students to examine their own note-taking habits. Ms. Washington introduced it to her students during the first week of classes and then spotlighted various aspects during subsequent class meetings during the first quarter. She started with the construction of the notes themselves, modeling effective note-taking behaviors during her classroom instruction. Within a few weeks, she was able to address how the notes should be used before and after class, even building in a few minutes of pre- and postreview time each day. "This proved to be the biggest game-changer for them," she said. "When they saw that reviewing and completing notes was valued in this class, they began to use them more often."

Ms. Washington has also changed the way she tests students on their knowledge. Each test is given in parts, and one section is devoted to open notes. This is her opportunity to ask questions of her students that require them to think critically. This is most often done through three short essay questions. Students choose two of the three to respond to and can consult their notes to construct their responses. "Of course there's information I want them to know without having to look it up, but that's mostly factual information," Ms. Washington said. "But I really want them to be able to think closely about how geography impacts human movement, culture, and conflict. It gives me a lot of satisfaction when I see them using their notebooks in such a meaningful way." And where did she find the self-assessment tool she uses with her students? "I found them with my notes from a methods class I took in my credential program years ago!"

Teaching Students How to Take Notes

No one taught our students how to take notes over the summer break. It is imperative that we teach them efficient note-taking strategies so they can

Figure 3.3 Assessment for Notes

	Never	Sometimes	Always
Prelecture			
1. I read assignments and review notes before my classes.			
2. I come to class with the necessary tools for taking notes (pen and ruled paper).			
3. I sit near the front of the class.			
4. My notes are organized by subjects in a loose-leaf notebook.			
5. I have a definite note-taking strategy.			
6. I adapt my note-taking for different classes.			
Lecture			
1. I use my pen in note-taking.			
2. I use only one side of the page in taking notes.			
3. I date each day's notes.			
4. I use my own words in writing notes.			
5. I use abbreviations whenever possible.			
6. My handwriting is legible for study at a later date.			
7. I can identify the main ideas in a lecture.			
8. I can identify details and examples for main ideas.			
9. I indent examples and details under main ideas to show their relationship.			
10. I leave enough space to resolve confusing ideas in the lecture.			
11. I ask questions to clarify confusing points in the lecture.			
12. I record the questions my classmates ask the lecturer.			
13. I am aware of instructor signals for important information.			
14. I can tell the difference between lecture and nonrelated anecdote.			
15. I take notes until my instructor dismisses class.			
Postlecture			
1. My notes represent the entire lecture.			
2. I review my notes immediately after class to make sure that they contain all the important points of the lecture and are legible.			
3. I underline important words and phrases in my notes.			

(continued)

Figure 3.3 Assessment for Notes (continued)

	Never	Sometimes	Always
4. I reduce my notes to jottings and cues for studying at a later date.			
5. I summarize the concepts and principles from each lecture in a paragraph.			
6. I recite from the jottings and cues in the recall column on a weekly basis.			
7. I use my notes to draw up practice questions in preparation for examinations.			
8. I ask classmates for help in understanding confusing points in the lecture.			
9. I use my notes to find ideas that need further explanation.			
10. I am completely satisfied with my note-taking in my courses.			
11. I can understand my notes when I study them later.			
12. I use the reading assignment to clarify ideas from the lecture.			

Note. From "Enhancing Students' Notetaking Through Training and Evaluation," by N.A. Stahl, J.R. King, & W.A. Henk, 1991, *Journal of Reading*, *34*(8), 614–622. Reprinted with permission of the International Reading Association. All rights reserved.

get the basics under control. When Nancy worked as a special education teacher supporting students with disabilities in general education middle school science classrooms, she would frequently model note-taking while the general education teacher taught. For 10 minutes or so, she would write notes on an overhead projector (and later a document camera) so that students could see how she was encoding the information she was seeing and hearing. From time to time, the science teacher would pause so that Nancy could explain her thinking about why she put certain information down, while skipping other facts. This gave her license to model how she would leave spaces in her notes so that she could later add more words. At other times, she would draw a simple diagram or add arrows or other symbols to connote relationships between ideas. The incidental benefit to other students in the class was a bonus and helped students see that taking notes was more than simply copying the words on the teacher's PowerPoint slides.

Watch Adam Renick talking about teaching note-taking at www.reading.org/ ch3_notes or scan the QR code.

The metacognitive nature of the Stahl et al. (1991) self-assessment as well as thinking aloud about note-taking is beneficial for developing student skills about making notes from text. In the same way that students must learn to summarize spoken materials, so must they do with written materials. Typically the notes they use in presentations and essays are the summaries of passages and whole articles.

Making Notes About Written Sources

Inexperienced writers often have difficulty writing efficient and accurate summaries of passages primarily because they don't know what to leave out and what to retain. Instead, they rewrite a nearly verbatim version of the original passage and inadvertently tread closer to plagiarism. Inaccurate notes about written work are problematic because errors are then replicated in the presentation or essay. Therefore, it is essential that students record the information correctly the first time so that errors can be prevented. Spatt (2011) recommends that students do the following:

1. Find a summarizing sentence within the passage (and, if you are using it in your own essay, put it in quotation marks); *or*
2. Combine elements within the passage into a new summarizing sentence; *or*
3. Write your own summarizing sentence.
4. Cite the author's name somewhere in the summary, and use quotation marks around any borrowed phrases. (p. 78)

This procedure can be demonstrated to students using the texts they are reading for content purposes. Consider this passage from *The Great Fire* (Murphy, 1995), a middle school text about the Great Chicago Fire:

> Chicago in 1871 was a city ready to burn. The city boasted having 59,500 buildings, many of them—such as the Courthouse and the Tribune Building— large and ornately decorated. The trouble was that about two-thirds of all these structures were made entirely of wood. Many of the remaining buildings (even the ones proclaimed to be "fireproof") looked solid, but were actually jerrybuilt affairs; the stone or brick exteriors hid wooden frames and floors,

all topped with highly flammable tar or shingle roofs. It was also a common practice to disguise wood as another kind of building material. The fancy exterior decorations on just about every building were carved from wood, then painted to look like stone or marble. Most churches had steeples that appeared to be solid from the street, but a closer inspection would reveal a wooden framework covered with cleverly painted copper or tin. (p. 18)

Now, a reasonable summary of the passage, with information conveyed accurately and without risking plagiarism:

> Jim Murphy, author of *The Great Fire* (1995), suggests that the city's wooden construction made the conditions for a fire more likely. He reported that a large number of Chicago's nearly 60,000 buildings were constructed mostly of wood and "then painted to look like stone or marble." In addition, the roofs of the buildings were finished with tar or shingles that were "highly flammable."

Well-developed notes that are constructed from the start with accurate attributions also serve as a way for students to repurpose them as part of longer pieces. We use a similar approach when writing summaries about longer articles. First developed by Cunningham (1982), GIST writing requires students to identify the main point in each segment of a longer text. Using the same process discussed previously, students write one or two sentences for each segment. Once completed, they have a series of sentences that begin to summarize the article. Ms. Schaefer used this technique after the close reading and discussion of the Stalin text. She segmented the reading into six sections and had students jointly compose a total of 6–12 sentences that accurately conveyed the information. Once written by the groups, the students then reread what they had written, searching now for information or ideas that were repeated (Spatt, 2011), eliminating or further consolidating the summary. Finally, they added information about the source and the purpose. Here is the summary of one group:

> In 1928, Soviet leader Josef Stalin delivered a speech to the Russian people on the need for industrialization in order to "overtake and outstrip" named capitalist countries such as Germany and France, as well as unnamed others. He spoke repeatedly his country being "encircled" and "surrounded" and warned that without technological advancements they would not be able to "achieve the final victory of socialism."

Once the written summary has been finalized, students are asked to record the name of source and author, page number, and bibliographical information needed. Instruction on written summaries should routinely follow close readings of texts that will be used in future presentations and written products. Written summaries are by far the most common kind of workplace writing that we do as adults. Summary writing instruction also builds the habit of locating and using textual evidence and provides students with written passages that can be converted into longer pieces. Keep in mind that writing often involves more than one text type, and these summaries make it possible for students to incorporate two or more text types in a longer piece.

Making Notes About Topics

So far, we have discussed note construction when information is furnished to the student, either in the form of classroom instruction or a text provided by the teacher. But sometimes preparation for a discussion or essay requires students to gather information. It is challenging to provide oversight and guidance for students when they are assembling information from texts, especially digital ones, that are not familiar to you. As well, it can be hard to determine whether the student is gathering a sufficient amount of quality information or instead is relying too much on a single source.

Helping students keep organized during the research process can be a juggling act. One tool that helps streamline this process is Diigo. A social bookmarking site, Diigo is browser based, meaning you can access the bookmarks from any computer or Internet device. In class and at home, students use the site to create individual research notes on webpages they find. Seventh grader Alvah, preparing for a research paper on extreme weather events in science class, started to look for information on hurricanes. He set up a Diigo group to bookmark hurricane articles as he searched. He was able to highlight important lines of text on the webpages and annotated his thoughts on the validity of the sources.

To help organize the information for his future paragraphs, Alvah created common tags for each page based on broad topics:

- Descriptions
- Causes
- Environmental impact
- Social impact

When Alvah came across the page about Hurricane Andrew, a devastating 1992 South Florida storm, he highlighted facts about weather conditions and wind speed, annotated a note on why this page was a valid source, and then tagged the page with the word *causes*.

He shared his Diigo group with his teacher during virtual conferences about the development of his resources. She was able to scroll down through all of his bookmarks and annotations in order to gain a sense of both the sources he was turning to as well as his emerging organizational structure for the paper. She made comments and asked questions on some of his annotations, and she bookmarked a few more pages he might find helpful. Having virtual access to his compiled research, a comprehensive organizational tool at his disposal, and feedback from his teacher gave Alvah the support he needed to succeed in writing his paper.

Preventing Plagiarism

"But the author says it better than I ever could!" Student writers are confronted with a blessing of riches. They have ready access to information in a few keystrokes. Literature that was once confined to the stacks of a brick and mortar library are now easily found in a digital one. Even better, the laborious and time-consuming effort of writing out a bundle of 3 × 5 notecards for research is no longer necessary. Highlight, cut, and paste into a document—voilà!

But the convenience of digital research and note-taking has made plagiarism more likely to occur. The speed with which one can locate, consume, and produce information can cause students to bypass the critical thinking one needs to use when considering how to most accurately represent the information. And limited understanding of plagiarism can lead students to overlook the nuances of a complex concept, leading them to justify their stance with claims like the aforementioned one.

What Is Plagiarism?

Most adolescents understand that the wholesale use of extended text written by someone else is dishonest and a clear violation of any school's academic honor code. Fortunately, those blatant attempts to pass off such work are relatively rare and easily detected. Teachers easily notice the use of a sophisticated sentence structure well beyond what is expected of the student writer. Or they see three different fonts being used in the same paper, a sure sign that there's been quite a bit of cutting and pasting going on. Suspicions aroused, it's easy to type a sentence into a search engine, place quote marks around it, and find several URLs that match.

But the meaning of plagiarism is both broader and deeper and may not be fully understood even by many teachers. Dictionary definitions link two concepts together: (1) using someone else's words, and (2) passing them off as one's own. But the assumption that the former is automatically the latter—a criminal act—is problematic. There is no U.S. legal statute that makes plagiarism a crime. Copyright law is designed to protect the rights, especially the financial ones, of copyright holders, but its 350 pages of documentation never use the term.

Watch Kelly Johnson talking about plagiarism at www.reading.org/ch3_plagiarism or scan the QR code.

Plagiarism extends to the use of ideas as well, and here's where it gets a bit trickier. As learners, students are novices at acquiring and organizing a cohesive set of concepts into a whole and are less able to determine the difference between intellectual property and widely held information. As well, some of our best teaching methods may unwittingly encourage violation of a narrow definition of plagiarism. We teach students to write using mentor texts and require budding artists and musicians to emulate the performances of masters in their fields of study. In point of fact, much of the process of learning is measured by one's ability to come as close as possible to imitating the thinking and performance of experts.

In their book *Pluralizing Plagiarism: Identities, Contexts, Pedagogies*, Howard and Robillard (2008) argue that a one-size-fits-all definition fails to recognize that a middle school student's cognitive ability and skills are quite different from those of a graduate student. They advocate for an agreement that in education "plagiarism is not a unitary phenomenon that can be successfully addressed from a single perspective…but must be considered from a variety of perspectives and a variety of sites" (p. 3). Like many other educators, we advocate for definitions of plagiarism that consider the developmental and cognitive needs of the students.

What Is Copyright?

The Copyright Act of 1976 and its subsequent amendments are designed to protect the proprietary works of writers, artists, and musicians from the misappropriation of their works for financial gain. It has been expanded to include newer forms of work and access to them and includes digital downloads and webcasts. As noted in the law, copyright has a constitutional link:

> The Congress shall have Power...To promote the Progress of Science and useful Arts, by securing for limited Times to Authors and Inventors the exclusive Right to their respective Writings and Discoveries. United States Constitution, Article I, Section 8. (U.S. Congress, 2009, p. ii)

The law attempts to balance the rights of the originator with the free exchange of ideas for the good of a society.

The issue of copyright is further complicated by the exception of fair use for educational purposes. Section 107 of the law states "for purposes such as criticism, comment, news reporting, teaching (including multiple copies for classroom use), scholarship, or research, is not an infringement of copyright" (p. 33). This doesn't replace the need to correctly cite information; however, it does make it possible for students and their teachers to make use of materials for classroom use. And pause to consider how often you have failed to cite information you have used in class. By adding the correct reference to the materials you use and distribute in class, you teach by example. This clearly communicates that you take citing sources seriously and practice it always.

Shifting Definitions

The concept of plagiarism has evolved in the last 300 years. Prior to that time, the idea that someone could "own" an idea was unheard of, a view that persists in many non-Western cultures even today (Howard & Robillard, 2008). The notion gained in popularity during the Industrial Revolution as a way to protect inventions, primarily through patent laws. Over time, these were expanded to include intellectual, literary, and artistic property, and plagiarism as a moral and ethical problem gained traction (Wikipedia, n.d.).

We cited Wikipedia quite deliberately in the previous sentence to highlight the way our definitions of plagiarism have changed with the availability of digital resources. Our own use of media clouds what constitutes plagiarism. The term *content scraping* describes the practice of copying content from one website into another. This often occurs with blogs and may or may not include the original source. But even our consumption of news further stretches what we have traditionally termed as plagiarism. Third-party news-gathering websites repost news from original sources, and although they usually cite the source, they use the content to create their own identity as a source themselves.

Digital sources continue to change, and with it comes our need to react to these newer sources of information. The American Psychological Association (APA), which is responsible for the style guidelines used in educational and scientific research, has had to add information to its 2010 publication manual to include instructions for referencing Facebook postings and Twitter feeds (APA, 2010). Given that definitions of how to correctly refer to digital sources continue to emerge, is it any wonder that secondary students have difficulty doing this well? Whether intentional, the complexity of knowing when and how to do so challenges us to respond to situations individually.

Unintentional Plagiarism

When we get right down to it and talk with students about the mistakes they have made, we find that students plagiarize for a number of reasons. We have talked with more than 100 students thus far in our careers about their "plagiarized" work and can cluster their reasons into a few main areas. Overall, there are students who do so intentionally and many more who do so unintentionally.

We'll start with students who plagiarize unintentionally. There is a small group of students who genuinely do not know that copying from the Internet is wrong. They believe that everything on the Internet is free and available for their use. To these students, they know that they cannot copy from a book but do not think the same rule applies to websites. This naïve assumption leads to some obviously plagiarized materials that are easily detected. Rather than punish these students, they need additional instruction focused on the appropriate use of electronic sources. We are reminded of Cesar, who was shocked to be having a conversation with a teacher about plagiarism. He said, "I have the book right there that I used." When confronted with the lines that were copied from a webpage, he added, "But that's not from the book. That is, how do you call it, common knowledge, because it is on the Internet."

Another group of students who plagiarize unintentionally do so because they do not know how to reference or cite their sources. We are reminded of Ashley, who had included a reference to a source she used but did not include quotation marks for the sections she used verbatim. In addition, she did not include the information in her reference section. She thought that including the web address in the introduction to her paper covered her for all uses of the information. As she said, "I said where I got it. See, right here," pointing to the website in the introduction. When asked about the quotes and the reference page, she said, "How do you do that? I never heard of that before." Again, students who end up plagiarizing because they do not know how to cite sources or include references need additional instruction, not punishments.

Intentional Plagiarism

The other major category of students who plagiarize are those who do so intentionally. Interestingly, it's not a devious as it might sound. The vast majority of students we have counseled in this category do so because they want to please an adult. In many cases, they lack the literacy skills to complete the assigned task, yet want to please their teachers by completing the assignments. We are reminded of Donovan, who finally confessed to intentional plagiarism. It took a while; at first he denied it all and even said, "I didn't take that. They just had the same words as me." When he finally understood that he wasn't going to fail the class and that he could save face and do the assignment again, he said, "Yeah, I guess I did that. But you wanna know something else? At least I cared enough. Like before, I wouldn't have even done the work. I wanna pass because you have really tried to help me and not let me just flunk and have to repeat." If that wasn't ever humbling and a clear cry for help, we do not know what is. Yes, Donovan needed additional instruction, but not about referencing. He needed help with his overall literacy, and we needed to modify some of his assignments so that he didn't feel the need to cheat.

Finally, there is a group of students who plagiarize even though they know it is wrong and they have the skills not to do so. When we talk with these students, they end up saying essentially the same thing: I'm lazy. When we talk further about this, we learn that they don't see the relevance in the assignments and they don't know why they're being asked to do the work of school. They don't care about the assignment, their grade, or something. Again, this falls on us. We have to ask ourselves, how can we make these assignments more relevant? How can we create learning tasks that invite students into the process so that they want to learn and want to attribute their sources correctly? Although there probably should be consequences for the students who willfully plagiarize, we do think it gives us reason to reflect on the assignments and how can we make them increasingly relevant for students.

Responding to Plagiarism

Given that there are a number of reasons that students plagiarize, how should teachers respond when they realize that a student has engaged in wrongdoing? In most cases, the response is going to involve teaching, which we discuss further in the section that follows. In addition to teaching students about plagiarism, we think that there needs to be a conversation with the student to convey the gravity of the situation. We like to have these conversations individually, and we present the student with concrete evidence from the source document. We do not like to accuse a student of unauthorized use of materials without evidence. We tend to start the conversation in a straightforward and honest way. For example, it is common for us to say, "The reason that I asked to talk with you relates to the work you have submitted. I'm concerned about your sources and the proper attribution of ideas and words. Here, let me show you what I'm seeing."

At this point, we show the student his or her work and the source information we have found. Sometimes, the student responds right away and admits to it and provides a reason. Other times, the student denies the accusation and we have to continue the conversation. We try not to debate the student; the evidence should speak for itself. What we do try to figure out is the root cause of the plagiarism so that we know how to proceed. For most students, our discussions lead to teaching points and students doing assignments again. In some cases, we have to involve the administrator and/or parents. This is especially true for students who are repeat offenders, which is almost never the case when we take a prevention and intervention approach to plagiarism.

The goal of the conversation is to have students accept responsibility for their actions and to learn from it. We want them to focus on the next right thing to do. In fact, we typically say it like this: "Now that you understand this, what is the next right thing you could do?"

This places ownership on the student. We do not force an apology because we know that students who are not ready for an apology only give a forced one and do not learn from it. We also know that students have to see how their actions have injured another person. What we have found is that most students think of plagiarism as a victimless crime, and thus do not understand our concern. As part of our "do the next right thing" conversation, we do talk about who has been harmed in the process—the teacher, the author, and the student himself or herself.

Preventing Plagiarism Through Teaching

As we have noted, there are a number of reasons that student plagiarize. For the majority of students, our responses to their transgressions involve teaching. Although there are times when disciplinary action is warranted, for example when students do not apply what they have learned in future assignments, the majority of our work in this area has focused on the instructional needs highlighted by students' inappropriate attributions to the ideas of others. We have found that modeling is critical to developing students' understanding. This can be done in any classroom. In addition, we have found that students need more detailed instruction about plagiarism in their English classrooms.

Teaching About Plagiarism Through Teacher Modeling

As with most other things that we want students to learn, we have to model for them. Students need to understand what is expected and how to do it. In other words, they need to see our thinking. Of course, students cannot literally see our thinking. Instead we have to describe how we do what we do. As Duffy (2003) pointed out, "The only way to model thinking is to talk about how to do it. That is, we provide a verbal description of the thinking one does or, more accurately, an *approximation* of the thinking involved" (p. 11).

We cannot simply tell students not to plagiarize and then catch them when they do. Instead, we have to provide examples of the thinking behind appropriate use of sources and how to attribute those sources. For example, Monica Cruise modeled writing a research paper for her students. As part of her modeling, she noted when she needed to reference and how she would include references. But the modeling was not limited to quotes and attributions. She also modeled her research process and her composing process. The key to modeling is that students are apprenticed into the thinking of another person, but that they do not have to exactly replicate the thinking of another.

For example, while looking up information about fitness and nutrition for her report, Ms. Cruise came across several useful websites. She was searching for information about serving sizes and nutritional value. She said,

> I'm thinking that there is probably a government agency that has to do with food quality and the health of people, so I typed in *site:gov nutrition* and got a great site called nutrition.gov that has a lot of useful information for me. I remember that I've used this type of search string before so that I can filter out sites that aren't developed by the government.
>
> For example, I see a link that says, "choosing healthy foods is more challenging for teens," and I remember that is one of the topics I'm interested in writing about. I'll click on that to see if there is more information that I need. [Reading aloud from the site] Oh, yes, this is evidence for the obesity issue with adolescents that I was writing about. I'm going to add this site to my references right now so that I don't forget. That's a mistake that I have made too many times before. If I don't get the reference information right away, and then I look at other sites, I forget where I found things and my references get all mixed up. Here are the authors, and a date, and the title. Excellent. I have that source added, but there might be more information that I can use.
>
> Oh, I see some really interesting information in the third paragraph. It's about sweetened beverages. Oh, yes, I think that I'm going to have to quote that for my paper. I think that the authors have a very good point and I like their words, so I am going to directly quote what they say. I'll add this on a notecard for now [opening a virtual notecard] so that I can use it later. Now I'll go back to the main page to see if there is other information that I need.

As part of her modeling, Ms. Cruise provided her students with examples of her thinking and the process she used to keep track of information that she would use for her paper. She added to her reference list and she decided that there were times when direct quotes could be used. She did not simply copy the quoted material into her paper, but rather saved that information for later and then continued her research.

A Guide to Style Guides

Student writers may encounter several methods of referencing sources during their research. However, students are usually taught one or two ways, and the formats can result in confusion. The most common one used in middle and high school is the Modern Language Association style, commonly referred to as MLA. This method is used in the fields of humanities and literature and is often the first kind students are taught in their English classrooms. However, this can be bewildering for students, who often face difficulty with knowing what to look for. A number of educational institutions have developed MLA study guides for students in grades 7–12. We especially like the one at the Oviatt Library at California State University-Northridge. It can be accessed at library.csun.edu/ egarcia/documents/mlacitationguide_highschool.pdf

Some students may also be taught the APA style for referencing. This is used in educational and scientific research, and students are often required to use this in college courses. It is useful for high school juniors and seniors to add this to their repertoire. An online tutorial of the basics of APA style can be found at www.apastyle.org/learn/tutorials/basics -tutorial.aspx and includes a 10-minute video. A third resource is the Purdue Online Writing Lab, which has dedicated resources for students and instructors in middle and high school. These include researching and writing up findings, as well as proper citations in either MLA or APA. These resources are at owl.english.purdue.edu/owl/resource/677/01/.

Plagiarism Unit in English

We begin each year with a two-week plagiarism unit in all English classes in order to establish foundational knowledge for students each year (Frey, Fisher, & Gonzalez, 2010). The unit begins with discussion about examples of copyright violations in music and fashion. Students listen to examples of sampling by listing to Coolio's "Gangsta's Paradise" and comparing it to Stevie Wonder's song "Pastime Paradise," and even discussing the use of a portion of a biblical psalm in the lyrics. They view side-by-side photographs of designer handbags and knockoffs, as well as counterfeit merchandise. The discussion then moves to examples of prescription medication counterfeits. In each case, the class and the teacher discuss who might be harmed.

In subsequent lessons, students read news articles about plagiarism in the popular press, as when reporters for *The New York Times* and *The Washington Post* did so in separate instances. They read an editorial about one such example, written by the ombudsman for the publication (the article can be retrieved at img.washingtonpost.com/opinions/the -damage-done-by-post-reporter-sari-horwitzs-plagiarism/2011/03/18/ ABgtIIs_story_1.html). In addition, students compare definitions from different sources on the definition of plagiarism, including the one used by their school or district. This establishes a context for the varying degrees of detail at the middle school, high school, college, and professional levels for both the definition and the consequences.

Using the appropriate style guide as source material, the next several lessons involve teaching proper methods for citation, referencing, and quoting. Many college libraries offer online tutorials to teach students the basics of plagiarism and proper citation. These can form a foundation for examining the bare bones of how and when to do so. Much work is done on paraphrasing, and the teacher models examples and nonexamples of each for his or her students. An effective means for getting students familiar with the mechanics of citation is to develop a scavenger hunt using the school's or district's style guide. The one used in our school is in an electronic format, and we install it on every computer in the school for easy reference. These lessons lead to students' first test on plagiarism, which becomes a good resource for later use should the need arise to have a follow-up conversation with the student about a possible incident.

Conclusion

When we prepare students with the skills necessary to focus on the discussion in a class, or pay attention to the details in a reading, we are equipping them with a life skill that they will use beyond the classroom walls. After all, how many of us continue to write directly on the texts we read and take notes during meetings or professional development sessions? It's not that note-taking and note-making are simply skills that middle school and high school teachers force on students but rather habits that educated people use to negotiate the world of information. With practice, students can transfer the skills they have learned—annotation, note-taking, and avoiding plagiarism—as they discuss their readings and write in response to the texts they have read. These skills have to be developed, through teacher modeling and student application, if students are going to be able to engage in the sophisticated thinking, discussing, and writing expected of educated citizens. Students must learn to read critically in order to question, analyze, and evaluate the information they are consuming. And, they must learn to provide evidence for their ideas and arguments if they are going to be taken seriously, whether that is in college or at work.

CHAPTER 4

Using Evidence in Discussion

Watch Nancy introducing the chapter at www.reading.org/ch4_intro or scan the QR code.

Tenth-grade biology teacher Liz Herrera uses annotation regularly to support discussion. She reproduced the text from her students' textbook so that they could write on the passage discussing transcription of DNA and RNA into the 64 amino acid codons formed through combinations of adenine, cytosine, guanine, and thymine, commonly referred to as A, C, G, and T. "This is a dense section of their textbook," she said, "and I really need to slow them down so we can unpack it. If they don't understand the A-G, C-T rule, they'll be completely lost when we start learning about nucleotides." Using an annotation protocol introduced during the first week of school, Ms. Herrera reminds students to circle unknown words and phrases, underline key sentences, and number steps in a process. As students read and annotate, Ms. Herrera circulates around the room with a copy of the passage on a clipboard. She observes the annotations students are making as they read and writes notes on her own copy. "I get a lot out of watching for the patterns of annotations I see," she explained. "This is valuable information for me as we move into the discussion phase." The words and phrases students select guide her selection of text-based questions she has prepared, and their ability or difficulty with identifying key sentences tells her where she needs to steer the discussion. "It's like I'm scouting out the territory so I can lead students to the destination," Ms. Herrera said, continuing:

> While I can make some predictions about what they'll have difficulty with, I have to say that every class is different. I can't just observe in first period and then facilitate the same discussion in every class. Otherwise, I'm in danger of overlooking what they really need to gain from the text.

In the previous chapter, we examined annotations primarily through the lens of students, especially in supporting their ability to prepare for discussions. But from Ms. Herrera's perspective, the patterns she observes as students annotate are important in her preparation for the discussion she will lead.

Classroom discussions should allow students to engage in purposeful talk, manage their use of academic and domain-specific language and concepts, and provide an opportunity for students to learn about themselves, each other, and the world. They must learn to do so in a variety of formats (including small group and whole class) and with a range of partners. Students should be prepared for these discussions in order to engage in thoughtful, well-reasoned discourse using evidence. In this chapter, we examine the role of discussion in classroom learning and how it can be employed to build the habits of using evidence and constructing arguments using reasoning.

The Teacher's Role in Leading Discussion About Texts

The teacher is the central operant when it comes to the quality of the discussion. Given the proper environment, students can and will discuss their perspectives in meaningful ways. However, students will not reach high levels of understanding in a classroom where the teacher is not skilled at, or committed to, facilitating discussion. Langer (1995) identified the following essential teacher dispositions for discussion (cited in Applebee, Langer, Nystrand, & Gamoran, 2003):

- Teachers treat all students as capable envisionment builders with important understandings and potential contributions to classroom discussion;
- Teachers use instructional activities such as discussion to develop understandings rather than to test what students already know;
- Teachers assume that questions are a natural part of the process of coming to understand new material, rather than an indication of failure to learn, and that questions provide productive starting points for discussion; and
- Teachers help students learn to examine multiple perspectives (from students, texts, and other voices) to enrich understanding rather than focusing on consensus interpretations. (p. 690)

Two important teacher behaviors elevate true discussion above more conventional Initiate-Respond-Evaluate (IRE) discourse that dominates so many classrooms (Cazden, 1988). The first is that the questions the teacher poses are not restricted to those that have only one "right" answer. The second is that the teacher regularly engages in dialogic instruction through uptake moves (Nystrand, Wu, Gamoran, Zeiser, & Long, 2003) that use student comments to formulate new questions (e.g., "Deka proposed an interesting idea about the limits of tolerance. How does the perspective of the author compare to the view she offered?"). IRE limits the use of evidence. Consider this exchange:

Teacher: "What's the meaning of the word *facile* in this text?"

Student: "It means something that's easy."

Teacher: "Right! What does *noisome* mean?"

The familiar exchange of this classroom question-and-answer routine limits student thinking by communicating that the teacher is interested only in a student's ability to replicate information. Although there is a place for acquiring foundational knowledge, IRE exchanges do not lend themselves to further discussion. In addition, they significantly limit the teacher's ability to uncover misconceptions or partial understandings of concepts. Consider the aforementioned example. This questioning exchange tells the teacher nothing about whether the student can speculate about why the author chose *facile* rather than *eloquent*. Although the initial question may be to check for understanding about a fact, the missed opportunity lies in the teacher's satisfaction with a low-level answer. Above all, because there is no entry point for evidence, the teacher has no idea where the information came from. In addition, it is a missed opportunity to foster metacognition with students.

Watch Aimee Suffridge talking about the value of student discussion at www.reading.org/ch4_discussion or scan the QR code.

Using Questions to Drive Text-Based Discussions

Complex text requires that readers act on it and maintain interaction with it. Readers of complex texts must generate questions as they read, mentally interrogating the text, the author, and the ideas posed. In other words, a conversation occurs. Readers ask themselves: Why this setting? Why this word? Why does this dialogue occur at this point in the text and not sooner or later?

In other words, students read like detectives. This requires that they zoom in on a sentence in the text for close inspection, and then zoom out to consider paragraphs, passages, and the text as a whole, across multiple texts. Because adolescent readers haven't yet fully developed this habit, teachers model and think aloud about how they formulate questions as they read. Teachers use guiding questions to assist students in approaching the text more purposefully. Most of all, they create opportunities for students to discuss the text at length with their peers.

As we have described in Chapter 2, these discussions require that students engage in multiple readings and that teachers use text-dependent questions to prompt students to return to the text. It is important to note that text-dependent questions should not be confined only to the literal meaning of the passage; although important, this does not fully capture the deeper meaning of the work. Therefore, text-dependent questions should also challenge students to examine the inferential levels of meaning, such as noting the mood and tone of a piece, or the author's purpose, or how the artful choice of words elevates the quality of the reading. These should be developed in advance of the lesson in order to ensure that the discussion regularly guides students back to the reading. Although the questions themselves move from literal to implicit levels of meaning, it is necessary to move between and among these types in order to guide students through a process of deconstructing the text in order to reconstruct it as a whole.

The discussions that follow readings are most effective when they require students to use textual evidence to support their statements. This is foundational to formal argumentation, as students apply rhetorical structures to written text. However, argumentation begins with its use in discussion. These start with asking students simple probes that follow the teacher's initial questions:

- Where did you find that?
- What does the author say that caused you to think that way?
- Are there other places in the text that lend support to your statement?
- Can you find an example?

These follow-up probes serve as a series of decision tasks, and when used consistently, remind students to look closely at the text to find evidence. By asking text-dependent questions and follow-up probes, students are more fully immersed in "what lies within the four corners of the text" (Coleman & Pimentel, 2012, p. 4). These queries are designed to encourage students to reexamine a text or passage they have read in order to extract essential information.

However, a narrow view of text-dependent questions can lead to an equally narrow view of what the text offers and what the reader expects of the experience. As we noted earlier in this chapter, text-dependent questions that require only low levels of comprehension will result in superficial comprehenders. Text-dependent questions that fall short of critical thinking will not build critical, or creative, thinkers. These questions should build a strong foundation of understanding of the text itself so that it can be used as a springboard to other texts, concepts, and topics. In this way, critical thinking becomes a habit of mind.

Meaningful questions gird classroom discussions but are limited in their effectiveness if only a handful of students participate. A shortcoming of whole-group discussion is that it seems like the same six students answer the majority of the questions. In order to overcome this, we interleave small-group discussions within the whole-class structure. After posing a text-dependent question, we direct students to locate information and discuss possible answers at their tables before bringing the discussion back to the whole class. As students work in their groups, we listen in on the conversations. Although not every student responds to the large group, the number of students willing to participate increases. As well, we know that the majority of them have participated in discussion at the small-group level. As we build capacity, we increase the frequency and length of peer-led discussions of text in the form of literature circles, jigsaw routines, and reciprocal teaching.

For example, when the conversation in a sixth-grade social studies class faltered, the teacher posed another question to jump-start the group. The students were reading a text about women's roles in ancient Troy and Sparta. They had been talking for several minutes about participating in the Olympics, and they understood from the text that women were not allowed to participate, even in these societies in which women had comparatively more rights than peers living in other places.

The teacher asked a strategic question to reengage her students in discussion, wondering aloud, "If they couldn't participate, surely they must have gone to watch the games, as spectators." Several students quickly caught on, realizing that the text actually said that women were not allowed to participate in the games, either as contestants or as spectators. As Jamal said to his group, "I think we missed this. We were all about being in the Olympics, but women weren't even allowed to watch." Marla added, "Oh, now this part later makes sense. It says that they sometimes dressed up as men to see their family members in the games. That's because they weren't allowed in."

Sophisticated readers understand that the nature of some texts requires that they be read more than once. Even with less dense text, it is essential to glean the details at both the explicit and implicit levels in order to fully understand the reading. So first and foremost, text-based discussions require a willingness to return to the text to read it more than once. The questions posed while discussing a reading are primarily text dependent and designed to construct opportunities to examine the text rather than simply draw on previous experiences that do little to forward new learning.

The Teacher's Conversational Moves in Discussion

Discussions can be difficult for some students to follow. The moves a teacher enacts during discussion provide a scaffold for organizing the information that emerges. In addition, skillful use of conversational moves by the teacher can propel the discussion, evoke reasoning, refocus attention on citing textual evidence, and clarify understanding. Taken together, these form the heart of accountable talk (Michaels, O'Connor, Hall, & Resnick, 2010). Over time, and with consistent daily opportunities to practice, these principles mark the way students engage in peer-led collaborative conversations. Michaels and colleagues (2010) recommend that teachers use the following conversational moves to promote accountable talk:

- *Marking:* "That's an important point." Throughout a discussion, important turning points occur, as when a speaker makes a pivotal observation that matches the learning goals of the teacher. Such a remark ensures that the point is sufficiently emphasized.

- *Challenging students:* "What do <u>you</u> think?" At times students may regress and direct questions to you that are better answered by other members of the class. Acknowledge the question and then repose it to the group to increase involvement.

- *Keeping the channels open*: "Did everyone hear that?" Statements such as this assist other students in building on the remarks of others.

- *Keeping everyone together*: "Who can repeat…?" Invite group members to restate important points in their own words, which emphasizes a key point, engages other students, and allows the original speaker to hear how his or her words are interpreted by another.

- *Linking contributions:* "Who wants to add on…?" Questions like this encourage cognitive connections within the conversation and foster investment in the discussion by recalling ideas put forth by earlier speakers.

- *Verifying and clarifying*: "So, are you saying…?" While the point may be apparent to the speaker, it may not be the case for other participants. Asking for verification provides all students with evidence or reasoning, and can expose a gap in logic for the speaker.

- *Pressing for accuracy*: "Where can we find that?" This probe refocuses students on the text, and can be useful when the discussion begins to drift.

- *Building on prior knowledge*: "How does this connect?" Link the concepts and texts under current discussion to those that have been read and discussed in previous lessons.

- *Pressing for reasoning*: "Why do you think that?" The intent of a question like this is to move the conversation from opinion to argument. This encourages the speaker to provide facts, cite textual evidence, or identify when the circumstance is ambiguous.

- *Expanding reasoning*: "Take your time; say more." This is a key probe in the teacher's cadre of discussion tools because it accomplishes so much. The most obvious is that it encourages the speaker to extend his or her response, but it also signals to the rest of the class just how much each and every member is valued. This deceptively simple move assures every student in the class that his or her ideas are worthy of the group's collective patience.

- *Recapping:* "What have we discovered?" Longer discussions yield ideas that evolve, and the questions that invite summary provide group members with succinct statements that heighten understanding. (pp. 27–32)

Watch Amy Miles talking about accountable talk at www.reading.org/ch4_talk or scan the QR code.

Accountable Talk Among Students

Accountable talk is an instructional approach designed to foster the meaningful conversation, respectful debate, and academic discourse needed to build the collective knowledge of its participants (Michaels et al., 2010). Accountability is threefold: everyone is accountable to the classroom community, to the knowledge base, and to reasoned logic. These discourse habits are built through teacher modeling and facilitation, with the intent of fostering application during peer-led academic discussion. One of the ways that we help students learn the language of accountable talk is through sentence frames. For example, the following frames were used to provide students with examples they could use when talking with their group members:

- I agree that ____, a point that needs emphasizing because so many people believe that ____.
- Though I concede that ____, I still insist that ____.
- While I don't agree that ____, I do recognize ____.
- The evidence shows that ____.
- My own view, however, is that ____.

We begin working on this habit during the first week of school, emphasizing ways that we report on the ideas of others and extend them with our own. We make a list of ways to do so, such as, "Can you put the author's ideas into your own words?" and "Tell me more about that." We then give students a discussion prompt and ask them to carry on a conversation with a partner where they encourage one another to elaborate on an idea. Pulling the whole group back together, we invite students to restate their partner's ideas. We then discuss the importance of listening, not just formulating one's own responses. By teaching discussion-based strategies such as accountable talk, students can learn to apply elements of argumentation in order to reach deeper levels of understanding in the company of peers.

During the second week, we spotlight lessons on accountability to the knowledge base. Because we're English teachers, we link this to the rhetorical structures expected when informing or persuading. Using a short piece of text, we analyze it for the writer's main points and identify his or her use of supportive evidence. We then ask partners to work similarly with a second short reading, usually an opinion piece such as whether zero tolerance policies are a good idea, and we encourage them to provide evidence of the author's claims for one another. We end the lesson with a discussion about the importance of being able to ask for justifications and evidence in our classroom as well.

By the end of the month, we are focused on the need to be able to present a reasoned argument without simply being argumentative. We list ways in which small children argue ("Ah huh"/"Na uh") and the pointlessness of such an approach. We then list ways that students can voice disagreement without shutting down the conversation. We introduce another topic for discussion and debate (e.g., uniforms in school) then ask partners to list the pros and cons. This gives them a chance to apply some of the strategies we discussed about voicing disagreement.

Using Classroom Routines to Promote Discussions

Group work routines that promote discussions focused on sharing include TTYPA ("turn to your partner and…"), as well as variations of Think-Write-Pair-Share that invite students to contemplate their perspectives and take into account the views of others. For example, 11th-grade chemistry teacher Tina Ye does this each time she posts a calculation: "We're figuring out acid-base titrations. Make sure to pay attention to how you're applying your scientific thinking in order to do so." After solving the problem, she asks students to check in with their lab partner. "Telling the other person your answer isn't enough. Explain your thinking and find out about how they solved the answer. If it's different than yours, dig even deeper." After a few minutes of paired discussion, students are primed for whole-class sharing. "They're often so unsure of their own thinking. They don't trust themselves yet. This gives them a chance to check in with someone else before we talk about it as a class," Ms. Ye said.

This technique builds on the partner talk we ask students to engage in throughout the year. We use Think-Pair-Square when posing questions that require deeper conversation. After partners discuss a question, they join another set of partners to square up and extend their ideas. Once the four students have met, we shift back to whole-class discussion of the topic. A benefit we find is that they become more adept at using features of accountable talk, especially in building on the ideas of one another.

Other routines require students to assemble into temporary groups for the purpose of sharing ideas and concepts. U.S. government teacher Greg Swanson uses Opinion Stations so that like-minded students can clarify their understandings and then engage with others who have opinions different from their own. He has posted four statements spaced far apart around his classroom: Strongly Agree, Agree, Disagree, and Strongly Disagree ("No neutrals in this class," he said. "Have an opinion, defend it, and listen to the opinions of others."). During a unit on legislative governance, he posted the proposed congressional redistricting map for their region and discussed some of the changes, then displayed a quote from the local newspaper's editorial section: "This process of redistricting has become a highly partisan tussle, at the expense of the voters of our county."

Without further discussion, he asks his students to move to the poster that best described their opinion. In the first round, the assembled groups discussed their shared point of view. After a few minutes, he then moved them to a second round of discussion, this time with members of another group with an opposing opinion. "I usually group the Strongly Agrees with the Disagrees, so they are not so far apart," he said later. After the second round of discussion, students can change their opinions. "That really is the process we should be used to in our government processes," he offered. "Open debate about the issues, with opportunities to change one's opinion based on discussion."

Text-based discussions need to be a regular feature of every classroom. However, the quality of the discussion is dependent on the level of preparation students engage in, in advance of the conversation. It is easy enough to give students a piece of text, ask them to read it once to themselves, and then react to the content. But a true text-based discussion requires students to look closely at the text in order to explore its ideas and not simply to lean back on prior knowledge and experiences. After all, the Common Core State Standards CCR Anchor Standard 1 in Speaking and Listening says, "Prepare for and participate effectively in a range of conversations and collaborations with diverse partners, building on others' ideas and expressing their own clearly and persuasively" (NGA Center & CCSSO, 2010a, p. 22). Starting in Grade 6, and continuing through high school, students should "Come to discussions prepared, having read or studied required material; explicitly draw on that preparation by referring to evidence on the topic, text, or issue to probe and reflect on ideas under discussion" (NGA Center & CCSSO, 2010a, p. 49).

Watch Aida Allen talking about the importance of student talk for English learners at www.reading.org/ch4_ELs or scan the QR code.

Building the Habit of Using Evidence

Many students are unaccustomed to furnishing evidence, and they may back down too quickly when pressed for it. All habits are built through repetition, practice, low-stakes attempts, and useful feedback. The starting point for getting students in the habit of thinking about evidence is through discussion. After all, evidence isn't going to somehow magically show up in their writing when they have had little experience using it throughout other aspects of their literacy day. In this portion of this chapter, we examine how teachers incorporate the use of evidence to build the habit.

English teacher Alberto Cruz uses Novel Ideas Only to get lots of examples of evidence out in the class in a short period of time. "I often have students working together to make a list of ideas," Mr. Cruz said. "But the sharing part can be kind of tedious, especially when the groups' answers are similar. We do this to promote more active listening." After reading the short story, "An Occurrence at Owl Creek Bridge" by Ambrose Pierce, groups met to discuss the characteristics of the protagonist, Peyton Farquhar. "As you make the list, be sure to cite where the text supports your answer," he tells them. After 10 minutes, the groups had generated nearly 50 examples. Many of these duplicated the work of other groups, so Mr. Cruz used this instructional routine as a way for the groups to report their findings. After asking all the students to stand, each group reported one example from their lists and crossed off items reported by other groups. As each list was exhausted, the groups sat down. Within a few minutes, 12 unique examples were shared and discussed, thereby eliminating the tedium of duplication.

Earth science teacher Holly Cohn frequently uses a Carousel discussion routine to foster the habit of using evidence. After groups work out a problem or question and record their ideas on chart paper, they rotate to view and discuss the other groups' charts, adding their own new ideas and observations to each chart. In order to ensure that the conversations don't become repetitive, she poses a unique initial question to each group. At the introduction of a unit on rocks and minerals, each group had a different question for their poster:

- What is our state's principal natural resource? Why do you say so?
- What is the rock cycle? Why do you say so?
- What are the differences between a rock and a mineral? Why do you say so?
- Does our state have more sedimentary, metamorphic, or igneous rock? Why do you say so?
- Where does soil come from? Why do you say so?

"This gets students thinking about some of the material that we'll be learning during this unit," Ms. Cohn said, "And it gives me a quick way of gauging their background knowledge. I can see the charts and listen to their conversations. And I can listen for their misconceptions, too." Her requirement of evidence to support each answer builds the scientific habits she wants to see them use. "It's not enough to just 'know.' You have to be able to explain and justify," she said.

Interactions like Novel Ideas Only and Carousel are essential for establishing the practice of listening and talking with one another about academic topics, as well as supplying evidence to support students' answers. The routine used by Ms. Cohn is geared primarily to building the habit of informing and explaining with evidence. Basic interaction routines occur throughout the school year and should not be limited to novice learners. After all, the need for students to share their thoughts and hear the ideas of others doesn't diminish with time and experience. But as students become more accomplished, it's time to challenge their thinking with evidence in argumentation as scaffolded by the teacher.

 Watch Yazmin Pineda talking about the importance of discussion for students with disabilities at www.reading.org/ch4_students or scan the QR code.

Strengthening Students' Capacity to Use Evidence in Discussion

Sustained student-led discussions must necessarily rest on evidence if they are to be productive. These require students to engage in extended discussions that mandate them to use argumentation. In other words, the discourse is elevated as groups exhibit a sustained focus on the problem at hand and a shared goal to resolve it. These include the following (Mitchell, 2001):

- Discussion centers on the evidence provided to the group.
- Claims that support the evidence are used by group members.
- The group returns to the evidence to review it.
- There is consideration of the positive and negative outcomes associated with the options proposed.
- Discussion is sustained for an extended period of time.
- Discussion is iterative and progressively advances toward the group's goal or stated purpose.

Each member of the group is individually accountable for his or her actions and contributions. These are higher stakes discussions (we call them productive group work) that focus more explicitly on resolution of a problem, so it makes sense that each participant should have a stake in the outcome. Three elements should be present: (1) the discussion requires argumentation, not just sharing; (2) the group's task is to resolve a problem, reach consensus, or identify a solution; and (3) there is individual as well as group accountability.

Discussion Roundtable. We were inspired by Burke's (2002) conversational roundtable as a method for fostering note-taking and the exchange of ideas. Rather than use a printed graphic organizer, we ask students to fold a paper in quarters, and then fold over the interior corner to form a rhombus in the center (see Figure 4.1). A group of four students jigsaw a reading, film clip, or other resource and take notes about his or her section. As they deconstruct the text, they note what each of the other three members had to say about their section. The center rhombus is devoted to an individual summary. Each student submits a conversation roundtable, giving us insight into both the group and individual accountability necessary in productive group work.

The applications are endless, as the four components can be assigned to reflect the discipline. For example, Reynaldo Guzman uses an adaptation of discussion roundtable routinely in his Algebra II course as a

Figure 4.1 Discussion Roundtable

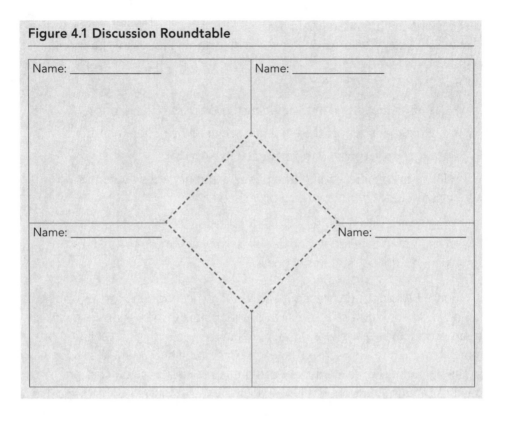

method for fostering note-taking as well as the exchange of ideas. "I post a problem on my interactive whiteboard and then ask students to move into groups of four," he said. "Each person folds a sheet of paper into four quadrants, then folds the inner corner into a triangle, where they will eventually write the solution." Each assumes responsibility for a specific role:

- Explain in words what the problem is asking you to do.
- Draw a visual representation of the problem.
- Propose an estimation of the solution and defend its reasonableness.
- Propose a method for checking the proposed solution.

Individual members of the group take the lead on their assigned conversation element, while the other members take notes and contribute ideas. After the group has completed the roundtable, they calculate the solution independently in the center of the page. Mr. Guzman invites a group to use a similar graphic on the interactive whiteboard to explain their mathematical thinking to the class. He said,

> By going through this process, really slowing down, they get the idea that it's as much about their thinking as it is about finding the 'right' answer. I really like it when another group realizes that they used a different path to get there.

Jigsaw. These same students regularly move through texts in other classes as well. Their U.S. history teacher Lee Nguyen often requires his students to jigsaw (Aronson, Bridgeman, & Geffner, 1978) longer and more complex documents. "We just did this last week when we examined the U.S. Constitution in detail," he remarked. "I can tell them what's in it, but I really need them to dive into it in order to understand its elements and how they relate to the whole." By dividing the class into expert groups that included the preamble, Bill of Rights, and individual amendments, students could first discuss their assigned section in depth with fellow learners who read the same section, and then present the information to their home groups later.

Text-Rendering Experience. Using the same document, eighth-grade social studies teacher Ray Wilkins uses a process called text-rendering experience (TRE) to locate the essence of the Bill of Rights section of the U.S. Constitution (Baron, 2007). "I have them use TRE when the document is dense, but the reading is fairly short," he said. Students read the document independently, and then review it a second time to mark their most meaningful sentence, phrase, and word. "There's no right answer," Mr. Wilkins reminds them. "Go with your gut." Students read the contents of the Bill of Rights in the U.S. Constitution first to get a sense of the overall document, then a second time to note their three choices. Working in groups of five, the students worked through the three rounds of the protocol found in Figure 4.2. Lexus's group identified the following phrases and words:

- Enjoy the right
- Right of the people
- Security of a free State

- Life or limb
- Freedom of speech
- Consent
- Peaceably
- Jeopardy
- Respecting
- Free

"The first thing I see is how much our list is about rights and freedoms," she said. "I guess that makes sense, 'cause it's the Bill of Rights and all." Oliver added, "But I think we also picked words that aren't about people fighting, like *peaceably* and *respecting*." For the next few minutes, the group discussed the intersection of rights and conflict, noting that "enjoying the right" was key. Mr. Wilkins then gathered all the groups together to continue the discussion. "You've had a chance to get some first impressions of the Bill of Rights," he said. "Now let's dive into them so we've got a better sense of what each means and what it means for society."

Figure 4.2 Text-Rendering Experience Protocol

1. Students read the text all the way through, then a second time to select a powerful sentence, phrase, and word. Each should come from a different part of the document.
2. Students work in collaborative groups and select a facilitator and a scribe. The facilitator manages the process while the scribe records the phrases and words identified. (Sentences are not recorded.)
3. *Round 1*: Each member reads his or her selected *sentence* with no further commentary by the individual or the group.
4. *Round 2*: Each member reads his or her selected *phrase* with no further commentary by the individual or the group. The scribe lists the phrase so that the group can see it.
5. *Round 3*: Each member reads his or her selected *word* with no further commentary by the individual or the group. The scribe lists the word so that the group can see it.
6. The members of the group discuss their impressions of the document on the basis of the sentences, phrases, and words that were stated.
7. The members of the group discuss new understandings of the document that have emerged.

Reciprocal Teaching. Physics teacher Thomasina Jackson uses reciprocal teaching (Palincsar & Brown, 1984) when her students read scientific articles: "They can get pretty complex, especially because they are often compact—an abstract, a short literature review, methods, findings, and discussion. And it's usually in an article that's only a few pages long." Groups of four students read and discuss the article in these chunks following an assigned structure:

- What questions do we have about this passage?
- What terms need to be clarified in order to understand this passage?
- How can we summarize this passage in a few sentences?
- Based on what we know so far, what do we expect to read about in the next passage?

"They need to make sure everyone understands it because they each write a précis about the article independently, with part of their grade derived from how well their group members do," Ms. Jackson said.

Watch Maria Grant discussing reciprocal teaching at www.reading.org/ ch4_reciprocal or scan the QR code.

Using Argumentation in Discussion

Argumentative text types must be understood by secondary students, but these are challenging to produce. In order for students to be able to create argumentative essays, they need experience with reading and discussing substantive topics that require them to think critically. Discussion webs, literature circles, and Socratic seminars provide students with frameworks for doing so.

Discussion Webs

"The secret is to give them something to talk about. There's nothing adolescents like better than a good controversy," says sixth-grade teacher Mike Alvarez. He values the role of collaborative learning in developing critical thinking skills for use in reading and writing. He begins by distributing a discussion web to foster meaningful conversation

(Alvermann, 1991; see Figure 4.3). This graphic organizer features a question in the center of the page: "Is the fast food industry responsible for the super-sizing of Americans?" Although some students are eager to answer immediately, he reminds them to first write responses supporting both a "yes" and "no" position in the columns labeled on the discussion web.

After a few minutes, Mr. Alvarez opens the question for discussion. Greg offers that Americans are getting fatter and Carmelita concurs, citing a news report she heard on television a few nights earlier. Elizabeth takes a different tack, explaining that in her opinion, people are responsible for their own health and no one is making them eat more food. Luz mentions a news story she heard about a man suing McDonald's because he was overweight. "It sounds like we have some pretty strong opinions but need more facts. Let's take a look at this reading for some more information," instructs Mr. Alvarez. With that, he offers a reading outlining some of the issues surrounding this controversy:

> I want you to read it for the purpose of collecting information both in support of the fast food industry's position as well as those of nutritionists. Don't just look for evidence that supports your own opinion. You've got to look at both sides of the argument. When you find something, jot it down on your discussion web.

As students read, Mr. Alvarez moves quietly around the table. He observes students annotating the reading and transferring facts to the discussion web and watches for signs of completion. "Now we have some more facts! Let's try to answer that question again. Is the fast food industry responsible for the super-sizing of Americans?" asks Mr. Alvarez.

A lively debate ensues as students alternately condemn and defend the fast food industry, citing facts from the reading. Mr. Alvarez returns to the discussion web one last time. "Please take a few minutes to review your notes. In the third section, add any points you heard during the discussion that you did not include originally." After the students have completed this task, he has one final set of instructions for them:

> You have the basis for an argument. Please use your notes to write one in support of either side of the issue. Remember to acknowledge the other position in your writing. I also have some additional materials for you to consult. They'll be in the independent reading section of the classroom if you'd like to choose them.

Figure 4.3 Discussion Web

Central Question:

Yes	No

BEFORE READING

AFTER READING

AFTER DISCUSSION

Be sure to cite your evidence!

Note. From "The Discussion Web: A Graphic Aid for Learning Across the Curriculum," by D.E. Alvermann, 1991, *The Reading Teacher, 45*(2), 92–99.

With that, these learners return to their desks, possessing the tools to write a compelling essay. Mr. Alvarez smiles to himself as he hears the debates continuing even as the students begin to write. "Like I said, there's nothing they like better than a good controversy!"

Literature Circles

In her high school American literature course, Karlene Palmer's students use an adapted version of literature circles (Daniels, 2002) in a way that is developmentally suitable for her adolescent students. She said,

> I adhere to some of the major principles, especially in ensuring choice from a list of texts I have identified. Early on, I form the group on the basis of their selections, but later in the year I will group them first and then press them to reach consensus on the text they will read.

Group members have a number of responsibilities, including creating a plan for reading the book, scheduling their meetings, and selecting the pages to be read between sessions:

> I don't give them assigned roles, such as 'discussion director' or 'illustrator,' as I find that these tend to inhibit the conversation. But I do teach them about the elements of argumentation in discourse and in writing, and they know this is an expectation of their discussions.

Individual accountability comes in the form of students' journal writing they conduct at the end of each session, as well as the literary criticism essay they write at the end of each reading. "It's hard to suddenly sit down and write in a rhetorical fashion when you've had little experience at doing so in discussion. These literature circle meetings give them the practice they need to read literature with a critical eye," states Ms. Palmer.

Socratic Seminar

As students become more comfortable with sustained discussion and analysis of texts, they are able to transition to Socratic seminar, defined as a "collaborative, intellectual dialogue facilitated with open-ended questions about the text" (Roberts & Billings, 2012, p. 22). Socratic seminar is one method for integrating speaking and listening, reading, and writing in a meaningful way. Students read and annotate the text in advance of the seminar in order to prepare for the discussion. This text preparation may occur within the classroom during lessons that lead up to the seminar, or outside of the classroom as students become more adept at analytic reading. Whether inside or outside of class, students write a short, reflective piece in advance of the Socratic seminar, addressing a question posed by the teacher. Such a question focuses on general understandings and key details, like asking students who have read the poem "Girl" by Jamaica Kincaid what can be surmised about the mother and her daughter. Deeper understanding of the poem, especially as it relates to themes, motifs, and historical and cultural contexts, emerge during the seminar.

There are several features unique to Socratic seminar, although many of the questioning techniques discussed in the previous sections are held in common. One difference is the length, which usually requires an entire class period, and sometimes two periods. Another is in the physical arrangement. The room is set in a circle or square so that all the participants can see one another. Each member comes to the seminar having already read and analyzed the text, as the focus is on deconstructing and reconstructing to reveal deeper meaning. The norms for discussion that have been used each day are posted and reviewed. Students who are new to Socratic seminar may need to be reminded that it is a conversation and, therefore, it is not necessary to raise one's hand. Although this may appear to be a minor point, it is needed in order to discourage speaking directly to and through the teacher, rather than the group. To further reinforce this norm, the teacher takes a seat in the circle, rather than standing apart from it. Other norms regarding civil discourse are essential, such as listening as an ally. Remind students that this is not a debate, and that the purpose is not simply to locate an answer. Instead, Socratic seminar is a forum for deepening one's understanding of the text and to entertain different interpretations. For this reason, texts that are somewhat ambiguous are excellent candidates for Socratic seminar.

The teacher's role is somewhat different during Socratic seminar, as he or she becomes the facilitator, rather than more directly orchestrating the conversation. For that reason, the teacher reacts only as needed to student responses, instead offering further questions to engage other students (e.g., "How would you respond to that, Jose?"). However, questions, and the strategic reengagement with questions, frame the entire seminar. An initial key question can be posed to begin the seminar and might be posted so as to easily return to it. Key questions should be open ended in that they are not easily answered, and they should invite interpretation. Possible opening interpretive questions include the following:

- What is the author's perspective, and how does this inform the message?
- Why is (word or phrase) pivotal to understanding this text?
- Is (concept) a good thing or a bad thing?

The opening question frames the rest of the seminar, which is furthered through the use of text-dependent questions that invite close examination of the text. The teacher continues to make publicly displayed notes for students in order to map the conversation and provide students with key points that can be used later in their analytic writing:

- What evidence in the text helps us understand whether the writer would agree or disagree with (concept)?
- What does (phrase or sentence) mean in the context of this reading?
- Where does the turning point in this piece occur, and why is it important?
- In what ways does our understanding of (character) depend on the (thoughts/actions/dialogue) of others?
- What is the theme of this text? What is your evidence?
- How does this text align or contrast with (previously read text)?

As the seminar comes to a close, the teacher/facilitator poses final questions that invite summary, synthesis, and evaluation. Examples of closing questions include the following:

- How does knowledge of this text inform our world today?
- Why has this text endured?
- What ideals or values are represented in this piece?

Reflection and writing continue after the seminar, as students reflect on their contributions to the discussion. In addition, the seminar sets the stage for more formal academic writing, as students now engage in literary critique and analysis. Having benefited from the input of peers, as well as witnessing how others have understood their ideas, students are better able to organize key ideas for use in their own writing.

Setting the Stage for Meaningful Discussions

Quality discussions don't just happen. Students need to be taught routines and rules for discussion such that they can exchange information and ideas with one another. Students don't arrive in our classrooms automatically knowing how to engage in text-based discussion or even being inclined to do so. It takes a skilled teacher to set the stage for meaning discussion:

- *Plan for purposeful talk* by incorporating standards, establish a clear purpose, and identify learning, language, and social objectives for lessons;
- *Create an environment that encourages academic discourse,* including the physical room arrangement, teach the routines of talk, and scaffold language;
- *Manage the academic discourse* through grouping and collaborative activities that increase confidence and provide students with ways to consolidate learning with their peers; and
- *Assess language development* using practical tools for monitoring progress and identifying areas of need. (Fisher, Frey, & Rothenberg, 2008, p. 2)

Conclusion

Meaningful discussions are essential for deep understanding of complex texts and ideas, but creating a culture for doing so can be challenging with adolescents. Remember the classroom scenes in *Dead Poets Society* when students were practically falling over their desks because they were so eager to offer profound statements? We've never had that happen in our classrooms. Instead, it takes a lot of work to make discussion happen. It begins with initiating discussion by developing a trusting climate for sharing ideas and with teaching routines and procedure that scaffold student talk. It is maintained through the use of text-based questions that prompt students to return to the text. And most important, the conversational moves of the teacher help us to refrain from telling them what to think and instead guiding them to co-constructed knowledge. Rather than initiate, respond, evaluate, let's initiate, maintain, and refrain from saying what we believe they instead can say. It is a truism in our profession: A good teacher tells you where to look, but not what to see.

CHAPTER 5

Writing From Sources

 Watch video of Doug introducing the chapter at www.reading.org/ch5_intro or scan the QR code.

The move from "conversation to composition" (Bereiter & Scardamalia, 1982, p. 1) means that at some point students must commit ideas to paper or screen. Hopefully, they aren't starting with a blank paper or screen. The benefit of repeated annotation during discussion of complex text becomes apparent when the time to write begins, as it provides students with something to write *from*. They also need something to write *about*, and a well-crafted writing assignment can provide students with a proper starting point. In this final chapter, we discuss the challenges faced by novice writers as they write from sources, elements of a solid writing task, and techniques for integrating source material into writing. We then examine the unique demands of writing from multiple sources. Finally, we discuss methods for revising and debriefing writing experiences with students.

Harder Than It Looks

We read for a variety of purposes—for enjoyment, to learn, to do something—but comparatively speaking, relatively little of our reading is specifically for the intention of writing. Yet, in school, much of the reading we ask students to do is meant to result in a written product. Flower (1990b) argues that this type of reading requires a specialized set of cognitive, social, and linguistic processes (see Figure 5.1). When faced with this task, students must read both as readers *and* as writers. In other words, they must find a way to align what it is they understand about the text with what it is understood about the writing task. The text itself resides in the middle, but the ways it is understood are influenced by the social context, discourse conventions, and language of the reader/writer.

116

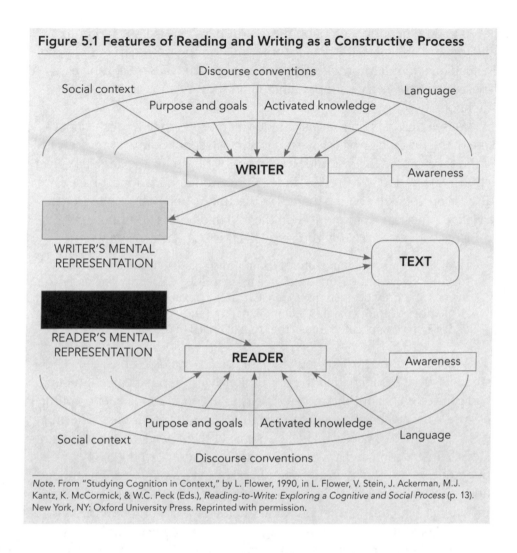

Figure 5.1 Features of Reading and Writing as a Constructive Process

Discourse conventions

Social context | Language

Purpose and goals | Activated knowledge

WRITER — Awareness

WRITER'S MENTAL REPRESENTATION

TEXT

READER'S MENTAL REPRESENTATION

READER — Awareness

Purpose and goals | Activated knowledge

Social context | Language

Discourse conventions

Note. From "Studying Cognition in Context," by L. Flower, 1990, in L. Flower, V. Stein, J. Ackerman, M.J. Kantz, K. McCormick, & W.C. Peck (Eds.), *Reading-to-Write: Exploring a Cognitive and Social Process* (p. 13). New York, NY: Oxford University Press. Reprinted with permission.

In addition, the reader/writer is considering the purpose and goals, as well as whatever knowledge is activated in the process of meaning making. This results in dual representations constructed by the reader and by the writer. When these are not aligned, trouble ensues.

A writing assignment or prompt should result, ideally, in the kind of writing one is seeking as a teacher. However, students interpret writing tasks quite differently from one another, and this variance influences the product (Flower, 1990a). Moreover, novice writers rely on prior knowledge of writing schemata and may not closely examine the task they are being asked to do. Therefore, although the assignment may ask the writer to analyze and interpret, the novice writer may simply summarize, focusing instead on a familiar format such as the ubiquitous five-paragraph essay. These schemata are not simply "untaught"; they must be confronted intentionally.

We see this happen routinely in our own 12th-grade English class. One of the first major pieces we taught in the school year was an analysis of the short story "Every Little Hurricane" by Sherman Alexie (1994). Over a three-day period, we used close reading, annotation, and text-based discussion, focusing on the themes of disruption and marginalization in a Native American community. On the fourth day, in a 90-minute period, students completed a 500-word essay in class using this prompt:

> How does our social and cultural community shape who we are? After reading "Every Little Hurricane" by Sherman Alexie, identify one or more themes and provide specific evidence from the text to support your analysis. Remember to apply insight by citing small but important details and then address the complicated issues that Alexie raises in the short story.

We were confident. We had taught a solid series of lessons, the students were engaged, and the discussions were sophisticated. Students had completed beautiful annotated texts to use in the construction of their essays. We watched our students carefully for signs of distress, offering quiet assistance as needed. The help some of them needed was surprising. Despite instruction and a writing prompt that were aligned, many of our students wanted to write personal responses. Keisha, a solid student and good writer, had begun her essay with a detailed discussion of the difficulties her cousin experienced in middle school. Although the task itself did not invite personal response, she had relied on a familiar writing schema. After all, hadn't she been encouraged for 12 years to write in this fashion? It was only after parsing the prompt and linking it to the lessons and her annotations was she able to develop a plan that more accurately addressed the task.

Flower (1990a) studied the reading-to-write processes of college freshmen in their composition courses. Students were tasked with reading an article on time management that offered conflicting evidence and to think aloud, transcribe, and analyze their thinking processes as they read and then planned their writing. Flower identified three strategies the students used. Many relied on what she called a "gist and list" approach, where they searched for the main idea and listed key points, staying focused only on what the text itself had to say about the topic, a strategy she described as "fast, efficient, and faithful to the source" (p. 235) but devoid of any construction of new knowledge. In essence, it's a synthesis or summary of an article but nothing more than that.

Other students, similar to Keisha, focused solely on personal response, or what Flower (1990a) termed *TIA* (True/Important/I Agree strategy). Although these students engaged in some evaluation, unlike the first group, theirs were confined to existing knowledge. In other words, they judged but did not question: "It is a one-way communication in which the student selects or rejects the claims of others but does not appear to listen to what the voice in the text is saying about them" (p. 236). This type of writing has its place as a personal response, and it can assist the writer in identifying an "organizing idea," but it does not challenge the writer to examine ideas that conflict with one's worldview.

Students in a third, much smaller group were able to leverage both of these habits—extracting evidence from the text and examining existing understandings—to question both the text and themselves. In other words, they transformed knowledge to reach new and original insights. Flower called this third approach *Dialogue*, as it described not only the interaction between text and reader, but also the critical thinking and writing necessary to engage in comparison, explication, reasoning, and contextualization of ideas. As Graff and Birkenstein (2010) note, academic writing requires that students engage in a series of moves, much like a conversation. In their words, "writing may require some degree of quiet and solitude" but writers can develop their arguments "not just by looking inward but by doing what they often do in a good conversation with friends and family—by listening carefully to what others are saying and engaging with their views" (p. xxvi). Table 5.1 summarizes Flower's (1990a) three reading-to-write strategies.

It is noteworthy that each of Flower's approaches has a place in the reading and writing diet of students. They become problematic, however, when there is a mismatch between the task facing the student writer and the approach she or he has selected to use. A well-designed writing assignment is a first step in helping students correctly match the task with the approach.

Table 5.1 Three Reading-to-Write Strategies

	Gist and List	True/Important/ I Agree (TIA)	Dialogue
Student's reading and writing behaviors	• Locating main ideas, themes, or arguments of the author • Identifying key details • Explaining the substantive message of the piece	• Identifying points of agreement • Dismissing or ignoring points of disagreement • Locating an organizing idea to use as a springboard for response	*Gist and List and TIA behaviors plus:* • Questioning the text and one's assumptions • Examining points of agreement and disagreement equally • Qualifying textual information with other sources • Building new knowledge on a foundation of existing knowledge
Focus	• Accurately conveying the information in the text	• The student writer's interpretation	• Constructing an argument using comparison, cause and effect, explication, reasoning, qualification, contextualization of ideas
Use of evidence	• Textual evidence to replicate knowledge	• Evidence is extracted from prior knowledge and experiences to comment on a text	• Textual evidence, prior knowledge, and the student's inferential understanding of the text to transform knowledge
Best for...	• Summaries • Précis writing	• Personal responses • Persuasive writing	• Analytic writing • Argumentation

Designing an Effective Writing Assignment or Prompt

A suitably designed writing assignment should guide students in developing their essay. As such, the basic components of a writing assignment or prompt are (a) the topic, (b) the audience, and (c) the rhetorical structure or genre to be produced. Oliver (1995) studied the effects of these prompt elements on the writing of middle and high school students, examining the interaction of audience, task, and rhetorical style to determine what worked best as writers developed. She found that middle school students did best when the prompt specified the audience, real or contrived, and when the topic statement was simpler (e.g., "Make a recommendation to a fellow seventh-grade student."). Ninth-grade writers were better equipped to handle more detailed information about the topic itself (e.g., "Discuss the causes and effects of water desalination on the marine ecology."), while 11th-grade writers in the study did best when information about the rhetorical structure was elaborated (e.g., "Select a position on the topic of stem cell research and write an argumentative essay that describes your position and offers counterarguments."). It should be noted that all three components—topic, audience, and rhetorical specification—should be present in a well-designed writing prompt. However, Oliver's findings provide more nuanced information about their relative weighting within a writing prompt.

A poorly designed writing prompt can result in student writing that does not meet the intended requirements of the teacher. Monte-Sano and De La Paz (2013) studied the effects on the writing of high school history students who were presented with one of four writing prompts that required them to analyze and write from two primary source documents (in this case, two speeches). Three of the four prompts resulted in evidence of historical reasoning while one did not. The prompts that required students to discuss the sources of the two documents, to compare and contrast them, or to consider the reasons why the speeches were delivered had a positive effect on students' historical thinking. However, the situated prompt that asked students to imagine themselves as a historical figure did not. Instead, students interjected personal opinions and used a contemporary lens when discussing events that occurred nearly 70 years earlier. Importantly, this last writing prompt had the effect of discouraging students to use evidence to support their claims, and led instead to them incorrectly foregrounding personal opinion and experience at the expense of analysis.

Skilled writers (a) establish their own writing goals; (b) use needed textual, rhetorical, or writing processes; and (c) are aware of the need to do both in order to write (Flower, 1990a). A good writing assignment or prompt should lend itself to this type of student analysis. Therefore, the student should be able to parse a writing assignment such that he or she can answer the following questions:

- What is my purpose for writing this piece?
- Who is my audience?
- What is the task?

The Literacy Design Collaborative (www.literacydesigncollaborative .org) proposes that good writing prompts can be formulated using prefabricated task templates that allow the teacher to customize. For example, the following argumentation task template invites students to compare two conditions:

> [Insert question] After reading _____ (literature or informational texts), write a/an _____ (essay or substitute) that compares _____ (content) and argues _____ (content). Be sure to support your position with evidence from the texts.

This template can be used as a springboard for writing in any number of subject areas. In each case, the writing task specifies the purpose and task in detail. We have augmented these prompts with explicitly stated information about audiences in order to further support students as they craft their pieces:

- *ELA*—What is courage in a time of war? After reading Stephen Crane's *Red Badge of Courage*, write an essay for peers that compares Henry Fleming's inner conflict and outward behavior as he wrestles with moral and ethical issues of war and argues for a definition of true courage. Be sure to support your position with evidence from the text.
- *U.S. History*—What is the cost of freedom? After reading *Korematsu v. United States*, 323 U.S. 214 (1944), the Supreme Court decision upholding the internment of Japanese and Japanese Americans during World War II, write an essay for fellow high school history students that compares the cases brought by the plaintiff and defendant and argues whether the court ruled rightly or wrongly on its constitutionality. Be sure to support your position with evidence from the text.
- *Science*—Is the expense of interplanetary exploration worth the cost? After reading the article "Mars Rover Curiosity's Siblings: A Short History of Landings on Alien Planets" by Clay Dillow, write a fact guide for potential voters that compares the knowledge gained with the cost in doing so and argues its worth to humankind. Be sure to support your position with evidence from the text.

The writing assignment or prompt should not be an afterthought, tacked on in haste to the end of a unit. Rather, reading and discussion tasks should be aligned with the culminating task itself so that students can more strategically engage in inquiry throughout the unit. As we have noted in previous chapters, the collection of textual evidence should begin with framing an investigative question, purpose, or problem to solve. In presenting a well-constructed writing task from the first day of instruction, learners are better able to assemble evidence for use in their formal writing. Further, as we have noted from our own experiences with students like Keisha, we must remember to teach our students how to parse these writing tasks such that they can select an approach that is well suited.

All of these examples involve extracting evidence from a single text source, which on its surface would seem to be a rather straightforward task. However, a common error many secondary students make is to focus on retelling the story or article, rather than addressing the prompt itself. These essays read more like book reports and less like evidence of critical thinking. They lack the ability to create a concise summary that accurately captures the most cogent information without devolving into a play-by-play recount of the plot points. In order to disrupt this pattern, we teach students about summary writing, which evolves into précis writing, a specialized form of summary writing.

Moving From Summary to Précis Writing

A major writing expectation of secondary students is the ability to write accurate and concise summaries. In fact, it can be argued that summary writing forms the basis of most academic and technical writing. Students write argumentative pieces that require supporting evidence, develop lab reports to describe the results of an experiment, and write informational essays on a variety of topics. Each requires the use of a series of summaries linked by rhetorical devices appropriate for the discipline, format, and audience.

Summary Writing

Inexperienced middle school writers may require more constraints on their writing in order to trim their analysis to the main points only. Teachers can use clips from television programs on topics of interest to the students to write these summaries. For instance, we played a 10-minute segment from the PBS special *Avalanche!* and discussed the main points (Frey, Fisher, & Hernandez, 2003). We then played it a second time, stopping at three points so that students could write one sentence (and one sentence only) stating the main point. After writing a total of three sentences, they revised and submitted a final brief summary of the segment. Short writing exercises like this build students' stamina and precision as they work toward crafting concise summaries. This technique is easily replicated in any content classroom that uses short videos.

As students become more experienced at writing summaries of video segments, they can be transitioned to short articles and text passages. Using the GIST technique proposed by Cunningham (1982), teachers read and discuss the content of the article, then segment the reading into manageable chunks, usually a paragraph or two each. The essential information in each text chunk is converted into one sentence. Therefore, a reading divided into five chunks must be represented in no more than five sentences. Students finalize their summaries and add them to their writing research notebook.

As students become more comfortable with the basics of summary writing, we begin to transition to more a formal type of academic summary writing, called the précis. As students amass a body of knowledge about a topic, they can begin to lose track of points made in earlier readings and discussions. This can pose a problem when developing the necessary evidence needed for the tasks that comprise many culminating writing assignments, especially those that are argumentative in nature. Teaching students how to compose précis writing develops their ability to understand the text more deeply, and to learn essential content.

Watch Oscar Corrigan talking about teaching summary writing at www.reading .org/ch5_summary or scan the QR code.

Précis Writing

This form of written summarization of an informational or argumentative text or passage requires students to distill the main points, "but also selecting, rejecting, and paraphrasing ideas" (Bromley, 1985, p. 407). The overall length should be about one sixth of the original, so that students do not sacrifice details for the sake of brevity. The text type should dictate the specific requirements. A précis for a persuasive piece should include the author's arguments and supporting evidence. The précis format is sometimes applied to narrative text, which does not usually contain an argument. However, there is a structure to an extended narrative. Therefore, a précis for a narrative piece should include the plot summary, rising and falling action, the climax, and the denouement. What is essential in précis writing of narrative or informational text is that it does not contain the student's opinions or questions, and it should not include any information not discussed in the text itself. These written summaries provide the teacher with formative assessment information about how well each student understood the text and whether additional teaching is required. For students, these précis writings cumulatively provide students with the information they need to assemble evidence they will need for their writing.

During a unit of study on short stories, Todd Cantor had his seventh-grade English students develop précis writings each time one was read and discussed. Short stories in this unit included O. Henry's "Gift of the Magi," Ambrose Bierce's "An Occurrence at Owl Creek Bridge," and Liam O'Flaherty's "The Sniper." In addition, students read several informational pieces on the history of short stories and the enduring popularity of short stories with surprise endings. Using the accumulated précis writings on the narrative and informational texts, students created written and multimedia presentations profiling a contemporary short story of their choice and comparing it with one they had read as a class.

Summary and précis writing serve as building blocks when writing from sources. Students must, though, also cite evidence directly from the text to substantiate an argument or illustrate an idea. However, the mechanics of how to do so elude many novice writers, who resort to clumsily and inaccurately paraphrasing, or directly quoting a portion of text without justifying its inclusion. The skillful placement of evidence in writing requires instruction on the art of paraphrasing and using direct quotations from the text.

Using a Paraphrase

Artful construction of a paraphrase is deceiving—it seems simple, but it is more complex than it appears. Paraphrasing is not simply substituting a few key words here and there while leaving the statement syntactically intact, as that is a form of plagiarism. Rather, a paraphrase is an accurate and complete representation of an author's ideas, in the order in which it was presented. The paraphrase is cited to signal the source, and the writer does not interpret or selectively omit inconvenient information that does not support one's claims. This can prove to be challenging for students who may wonder what the difference is between a summary and a paraphrase—and, in fact, they are quite similar. Spatt (2011) compares and contrasts the two techniques in Table 5.2.

As with most other things that we want students to learn, we have to model paraphrasing for them. Students need to understand what is expected and how to do it. In other words, they need to see their teachers' thinking. Of course, students cannot literally see thinking. Instead, teachers have to describe how they do what we do. As Duffy (2003) pointed out, "The only way to model thinking is to talk about how to do it. That is, we provide a verbal description of the thinking one does or, more accurately, an *approximation* of the thinking involved" (p. 11).

Modeling allows teachers to provide examples of the thinking behind appropriate use of sources and how to attribute those sources. For example, ninth-grade English teacher Tom Mitchell modeled paraphrasing for a research paper his students would be writing. As part of his modeling, he noted when he needed to reference and how he would include references. But the modeling was not limited to quotes and attributions. He also modeled his research and composing processes using a think-aloud method:

> So I've figured out that I want to paraphrase [Anna] Quindlen's discussion of tolerance in "A Quilt for a Country" in my paper. But I see that I don't need

Table 5.2 Comparing Paraphrase and Summary

Paraphrase	Summary
• Reports your understanding to your reader	• Reports your understanding to your reader
• Records a relatively short passage	• Records a passage of any length
• Records every point in the passage	• Selects and condenses, recording only main ideas
• Records the points in their original order	• Changes the order of ideas when necessary
• Includes no interpretation	• Explains and (if the writer wishes) interprets

Note. From *Writing From Sources*, 8th ed., (p. 152), by B. Spatt, 2011, Boston, MA: Bedford/St. Martin's. Reprinted with permission.

a direct quote because it would be really long and I'm sure I can make the same point in my own words. So I'm going to highlight and number the ideas she had in this paragraph and list them in my notes. But I'm also going to be careful not to write down her exact words, because I'm paraphrasing.

As he lists the phrases using the document camera, he explains his reasoning for selecting each one. By including his thoughts, Mr. Mitchell is going beyond demonstration, in which cognitive processes are hidden, to a true think-aloud. For example, he says:

> She says that "Tolerance is a word used most often when this kind of coexistence exists; but tolerance is a vanilla-pudding word, standing for little more than the allowance of letting others live unremarked and unmolested." She has three ideas here: One is that the word *tolerance* gets used more often when diverse people live in close proximity. The second is that it's too bland for her liking. The third is connected to the second. She says tolerance is just a thin disguise for giving permission and little more for someone to be. So I'll put those three ideas together: "In Quindlen's (2001) view, the word *tolerance* is a bland and thinly disguised term that allows people to be, but little more than that."

As part of his modeling, Mr. Mitchell provided his students with examples of his thinking and the process he used to keep track of information. He added the citation to the reference list so he would have it for future use. By regularly modeling paraphrasing using portions of texts they were reading, Mr. Mitchell's students became accustomed to the method. In addition, they include discussion of how the writers they read use paraphrasing techniques in their own works. "They need to see how writers use this technique, and how they incorporate paraphrasing smoothly into texts. I've never had a 'paraphrasing unit' because they wouldn't have a chance to generalize this," he said. "I'd rather have them notice how the technique is developed and used by writers, including myself."

Watch Sarah Soriano talking about the value of modeling for students with disabilities at www.reading.org/ch5_modeling or scan the QR code.

Using Direct Quotations

Compared with paraphrasing, the use of direct quotations may seem apparent. After all, it's just about getting the words down accurately and citing it correctly, right? Although those two conditions are true, neither goes far enough in explaining how this technique is done in a skillful manner. Fortunately, the texts students read and discuss are filled with quotes and can provide adolescent writers with models for doing so themselves.

Style manuals are filled with information about how to correctly cite a direct quote, but they give comparatively little information about the decision making that accompanies the placement of a quote. Spatt (2011) offers three reasons for using a direct quotation in an essay:

1. To gain support by quoting an expert, eyewitness, or other authority.

2. To capture vivid or technical language that would otherwise be diminished through paraphrasing.

3. To gain distance from a position or argument by separating oneself from the source being quoted.

Direct quotations can be stand-alone, meaning that they are used in their entirety and function separately from the writer's own words: In Harper Lee's (1960/2002) *To Kill a Mockingbird*, Scout says that her Aunt Alexandra disapproved of her dress and demeanor. "I was born good but had grown progressively worse every year" (p. 108). Later in the same essay, the writer integrates a partial quote into her writing: Atticus had told the children that "'It's a sin to kill a mockingbird,' explaining that the creature exists only to bring joy and does no harm" (p. 119).

The mechanics of using stand-alone and integrated quotes are mastered fairly quickly when explicitly taught and used. However, novice writers may believe that the quotation alone explains all and requires no further explication. Thus, they will end a paragraph or section of an essay with the quote, leaving the reader to deduce why this is significant. As in discussion, student writers need to couple evidence (the quote) with reasoning (the rationale):

> Once you have presented a quotation, you need not provide an exact repetition of the same idea in your own words, making the same point twice. Instead, follow up a quotation with an *explanation* of its relevance to your paragraph or an *interpretation* of its meaning. (Spatt, 2011, p. 139)

In the same way that we use "because" in discussion, a paraphrase or direct quotation needs to be supported by a justification that lays out a reason for its placement in the paper.

Linking quotes to reasoning is challenging for any writer, especially for novice writers. Jago (2002), an experienced high school English teacher herself, asks her student writers who struggle to make the connection between evidences in the text and their analysis to complete a four-column exercise:

- Quote from the chapter (including page number).
- What I think.
- What this says about the text.
- What this says about the world. (p. 75)

Eighth-grade student Pablo completed the exercise while reading Jack London's (1906/2003) *White Fang*:

- *Quote from the chapter*—"The aim of life was meat. Life itself was meat. Life lived on life. There were the eaters and the eaten. The law was: EAT OR BE EATEN. He did not formulate the law in clear, set terms and moralize about it. He did not even think the law; he merely lived the law without thinking about it at all." (p. 153)
- *What I think*—White Fang is remembering when he was a cub and he hunted with his mother. He is learning that all animals are eaters or they are eaten.
- *What this says about the text*—He is not upset by this. It is just the way his life is, and he is not going to question it.
- *What this says about the world*—This makes me think about the law of the jungle or the circle of life. It isn't good or bad. It just is.

Pablo and his peers write these notes in their journals for use later as they write their literary analysis. Before that time, he will have used these notes as part of discussions and had the opportunity to expand them on the basis of the insights of others. His teacher, Ruth Quiroz, said,

> I want to make sure they aren't beginning an essay with nothing to work from. By the time they are ready to compose, they should already have components of the essay completed. The "quote notes" are important because it builds the habit of using direct evidence and explaining why the evidence supports their ideas.

Framing for Reluctant Writers

Even with sound instruction, modeled writing, attention to writer's craft in the texts they read, and brief writing to be used later in formal essays, some students still have difficulty getting started. For some students, assistance comes in the form of parsing the writing assignment itself. As discussed earlier in this chapter, a well-developed writing assignment should provide the information students need to answer three questions: What is my purpose for writing this piece? Who is my audience? What is the task? Students who have trouble getting started may need only to be guided through these three questions to clarify. But for others, it is the thesis statement itself that is the roadblock. They just can't seem to get their heads around a good idea.

Watch Ashlee Montferret talking about support for reluctant writers at www.reading.org/ch5_support or scan the QR code.

The development of a thesis statement is difficult for many students because, frankly, it requires a lot of thinking. When a student is stuck, the teacher tries to help by looking back through the student's notes, asking him or her to identify patterns. A pad of sticky notes is useful. To provide this level of support, the teacher has to sit with the student as she or he writes one idea or concept on each note. Then the student should be helping to sort these notes into categories. Once completed, the categories can be labeled. Often, the student starts drawing conclusions and synthesizing information even before he or she is finished creating notes. It seems like the physical act of sorting and categorizing brings order to a jumbled mind. This isn't a technique reserved only for novice writers; we often use the same method to organize our writing.

There are times when the sorting activity isn't sufficient, and the student needs further guidance. We use a technique developed by Flower (1993) called *nutshelling*. The aim of nutshelling is to assist struggling writers in distilling their ideas. Students write for several minutes about one of the categories they have developed from the sorting activity, and then reread their writing. They then compose one sentence that represents the content of the first round of writing "in a nutshell," so to speak. They write for several more minutes using the nutshell sentence as the first, and then repeat the process again. It's similar to the GIST technique used for summary writing, except this time students use their own compositions. It is true that leading an individual student through sorting and nutshelling is time-consuming.

However, we have witnessed some writers do this for themselves on their own on future writing assignments. The truth is, we all get stuck when writing. Having some techniques for getting yourself unstuck can mean the difference between a blank page and a completed task.

Thus far, we have focused on writing from a single text source, but many writing tasks incorporate two or more pieces. This certainly ups the stakes for students who must identify patterns and apply critical thinking skills across multiple documents. In the next section, we examine the unique challenges of writing from several sources.

Writing Across Multiple Texts

The challenge of reading in this century isn't in finding information—it's figuring out how to consolidate all this readily available information in ways that facilitate understanding (Goldman, 2004). Certainly students' search habits have much to do with this, and most students are able to locate a multitude of resources with a few keystrokes. But students remain challenged about how to synthesize disparate information, especially when it is contradictory. As well, although many can distill a single reading, most can't effectively use multiple texts to strengthen arguments.

Consider just how difficult it is, even for a strong reader, to turn disparate documents into a coherent set of information. As readers, we rely on the author to link concepts within a single piece of text (Goldman & Rakestraw, 2000). Authors typically use connectives such as *because* and *however*, place main ideas at the beginning of a paragraph to enhance comprehension, and provide transitional phrases such as *in summary* to signal organizational shifts. But no such devices bridge multiple documents. A reader must construct meaning for herself by building organizational bridges that cross the divide between texts. There simply is no one there to do that for her. Other factors that make reading multiple texts more difficult include differences in the writing styles used by different authors, competing perspectives and interpretations, and even the chronology of when the documents were created.

Most of us have experienced this in our own lives, such as when we try to distill information about a medical condition from an Internet search. Like our students, we are novices in regard to the content, and figuring out how to best treat that stuffy nose and sore throat we're suffering from isn't helped when reading so much conflicting advice (Starve a cold and feed a fever?). Without the ability to evaluate the source of the information, identify areas of corroboration and disagreement, and make decisions about what to ignore and what to pursue, we cannot take action. We're left feeling confused and no better off than when we started.

The ability to read and write from multiple texts has implications for testing and accountability as well. A looming challenge lies in the suite of assessments currently being developed by the Smarter Balanced Assessment Consortium and the Partnership for Assessment of Readiness for College and Careers. Forty-six states belong to one of these consortia that are charged with developing measurement systems aligned with the CCSS. The English language arts and content literacy standards refer repeatedly to the expectation that students can manipulate information across texts and platforms. Writing Anchor Standard 8 illustrates this point: "Gather relevant information from multiple print and digital sources, assess the credibility and accuracy of each source, and integrate the information while avoiding plagiarism" (NGA Center & CCSSO, 2010a, p. 41). Keep in mind that "print and digital sources" refer not only to written texts, but also to video, sound recordings, charts, diagrams, and photographs.

Fostering Comprehension of Multiple Texts

Literary, informational, and persuasive texts don't exist in a vacuum. They were written by someone for a particular purpose, at a specific time, for a designated audience. To understand a text is to know that these dimensions matter. As discussed in Chapter 1, history educator Wineburg (1991) refers to the practice of identifying these as *sourcing* and *contextualizing*. Sourcing a text requires students to examine the publication date and the author's biographical statement, for instance. Texts are further contextualized by locating the writing within a time period, determining the purpose, and identifying the audience for whom it was intended.

Notice that we're not discussing the simpler forms of reading comprehension—determining main ideas and such—but rather linking what occurs within the page to the social, biological, or material world. Importantly, we are also not describing the serial reading of lots of texts with no opportunity to figure out how they intersect. Multiple-text comprehension does something important to the mind; it links reading to reasoning. The Documents Model framework describes comprehension across texts as a series of mental representations that move from understanding them singly to formulating conclusions drawn from multiple pieces (Perfetti, Rouet, & Britt, 1999):

1. Initially, students focus on the content of a single text, moving to sourcing and contextualizing through rereading and text-dependent questions designed to prompt discussion.

2. They repeat this process with a second piece of text, including rereading and discussion. Now questions are used to guide student thinking about *intertext* processes. Are the documents in agreement with one another? How do they differ? Does the information from one corroborate with or expand on the information of the other?

3. Moving forward, students are challenged to form an *integrated mental model* in which they must decide what information must be discounted or ignored, what information overlaps and is therefore corroborated, and what is unique but credible.

4. These processes are driven by *tasks* that require students to synthesize information from more than one piece of text. Often, these come in the form of a written or oral assignment.

There is a growing body of evidence that the quality of the task questions can either foster or inhibit a student's ability to write critically in history (Monte-Sano & De La Paz, 2012) and to engage in argumentation in science (Chin & Osborne, 2010).

Getting Started: Creating Experiences With Multiple Texts

Let's face it—as secondary educators, we rarely use multiple pieces of text for teaching content. Most assigned reading comes from the textbook or anthology and is often "one and done." In other words, students rarely consult a text once they have read it through a single time. This is what makes close reading so unfamiliar, because teachers and students historically don't routinely linger on a piece. To be sure, some readings are simple enough that they don't warrant such careful inspection. But many of the readings used in classrooms would be excellent candidates for the kind of repeated reading and discussion that is driven by text-dependent questions. These practices, and the habits of mind that accompany them, are foundational for understanding multiple texts.

Another barrier is our own familiar instructional practices. We rarely bring back a previously taught piece in order to compare it with another. In order for students to develop the skills they need to compare information and ideas across texts, they must regularly revisit them. It isn't always necessary for students to be confronted with two or more unfamiliar readings all at once. Building the comparative skills to process concepts is likely to mean that students use a known piece of text to understand a new reading. U.S. government teacher Sheryl Segal did just that a few days after the 2012 presidential election. She resurrected a familiar piece that her 12th-grade students had learned earlier in the semester, the famous "Four Freedoms" speech delivered by President Franklin Delano Roosevelt to the U.S. Congress in 1941. Her students had previously learned that Roosevelt described four goals: freedom of speech and expression, freedom of worship, freedom from want, and freedom from fear. His purpose, they had determined, was to rally public support for an impending war by placing pressure on the politicians. Even though he was addressing Congress, his real audience was the American public.

Ms. Segal brought back a portion of President Roosevelt's speech for students to use to examine the acceptance speech President Barack Obama gave the night of the election. Using the text of the 2012 speech, they first read and discussed the major ideas, noting that the goals included congratulating his opponent, thanking his supporters, and outlining an agenda for next steps. Ms. Segal then distributed a graphic organizer with Roosevelt's four freedoms listed, as well as another concept: "We have been engaged in change—in a perpetual peaceful revolution" (Roosevelt, 1941). Students reread President Obama's speech and annotated the text when statements made in 2012 echoed the ideas put forward by President Roosevelt in 1941. Students recorded these quotes on the graphic organizer (see Figure 5.2 for one student's notes). The comparison of the two documents illuminated another concept students had not initially perceived. "Now I'm thinking about the similarities between the two times," said Simone. "Everyone's always talking about the economy and about international terrorism and wars because those are in the news every day," she said, continuing:

> But it's really not so different from 1941. People then were worried about the Great Depression and the fact that the economy was so bad for so long. And

Figure 5.2 Student's Analysis of Two Speeches

Freedom of Speech and Expression	Freedom of Worship	Freedom From Want	Freedom From Fear
• "Whether you held an Obama sign or a Romney sign, you made your voice heard" • "Working late in a campaign office" • "We have our own opinions… and beliefs" • "We will disagree, sometimes fiercely about how to get there" • "As it has for two centuries, progress will come in fits and starts"	• "Freedom and dignity for every human being" • "A tolerant America" • "With your help and God's grace" • "God bless you" • "God bless these United States"	• Every child has the chance to go to college • "Access to the best teachers and schools" • "Good jobs and new businesses" • "A nation that isn't burdened by debt" • "A generous America" • "A compassionate America" • "Open to the dreams of an immigrant daughter who studies in our schools and pledges to our flag" • "Our economy is recovering"	• "The destructive power of a warming planet" • "A country that's safe and respected and admired around the world" • "A nation that is defended by the strongest military on Earth and the best troops" • "A decade of war is ending"

"Perpetual Peaceful Revolution"

"More than 200 years after a former colony won the right to determine its own destiny, the task of perfecting our union moves forward."

"We are an American family and we rise or fall together as one nation and one people."

"Democracy in a nation of 300 million can be noisy and messy and complicated."

"The painstaking work of building consensus and making difficult compromises needed to move this country forward."

"The role of citizens in our Democracy does not end with your vote… it's about what can be done by us together through the hard and frustrating, but necessary work of self-government."

then there was Hitler and Mussolini and Hirohito that were doing so many awful things in Europe and Asia. Scary, right?

Simone said, "It's not so different today. A president trying to persuade the people and the Congress that we need to remember our founding principles to improve our economy and our safety."

Teach That Knowledge Is Complex

As noted earlier, the ability to synthesize information across multiple documents is not confined to reading comprehension. A student's belief about knowledge is also critical. Bråten and Strømsø (2010) examined the ways in which undergraduates made sense from several documents containing conflicting information. They found that those students who held a simplistic view of knowledge, that is, one that was relatively fixed, unchanging, and held by an outside authority, were poorer comprehenders of the documents. The authors stated that

> Not surprisingly, students tending to believe that knowledge consists of highly interrelated concepts seem better able to handle documents expressing diverse and even contradictory ideas than students tending to believe that knowledge consists of an accumulation of isolated facts. (p. 638)

This is an important consideration for science teachers. Students often approach science documents as being fixed and absolute, with little room for debate. But debate and disagreement are at the heart of science. Multiple interpretations of data are often necessary in order to derive theoretical constructs, and the ability to engage in speculation, formulate hypotheses, and propose solutions replicates what scientists do (Wellington & Osborne, 2001). As members of the public, we witness these debates in such diverse topics as climate change, gene therapy, nuclear energy, and deep space exploration.

Seventh-grade physical science teacher Edward Margate used multiple documents to examine the future of the space exploration program in the United States. Over the course of two class periods, students watched film clips of President John F. Kennedy promising in 1961 that there would be a man on the moon before the decade ended, as well as newscasts of tragedies such as the 1967 fire that killed three astronauts and the space shuttle explosions in 1986 and 2003. Students read a newspaper editorial projecting the expenditures of NASA until 2020, an article detailing the products and technologies derived from the space program, and a letter authored by astronaut Neil Armstrong to President Obama in 2010 asking him to reconsider his decision to cancel the Constellation human spaceflight program.

"The task was really important in this case," said Mr. Margate. "Students had to plow through a lot of information and weigh the evidence to support their opinions." His students worked in small groups to prepare their arguments, using evidence from texts to support their claims. The science teacher provided his students with a graphic organizer to foster intertextual connections and to construct mental models through the use of a discussion web (Alvermann, 1991). "I altered it a bit so that students would always keep both sides of the argument in mind," he said. "I wanted them to appreciate that these are complex issues to wrestle with. It's a chance for them to put their scientific literacy to good use."

Watch Broc Arnaiz talking about the difference between writing from one source and from multiple sources at www.reading.org/ch5_source or scan the QR code.

Teach Causal Relationships to Promote Connections

As educators, we teach for conceptual connections all the time. In fact, the ability to perceive relationships between and among principles, theories, and themes is a mark of a learner's sophistication. No matter the content we teach, we ensure that our students see these links. For instance, we use graphic organizers and concept maps as visual representations of these cognitive connections. But when confronted with locating these links across texts, many students have difficulty with seeing the relationships between documents, treating them as silos housing discrete information.

A study of middle school social studies students illustrates this point. During a unit on the Montgomery Bus Boycott during the Civil Rights movement, those who were explicitly taught causal connections between events were better able to locate and recall this information across multiple sources, including primary source documents, a documentary, and readings from their textbooks (Espin, Cevasco, van den Broek, Baker, & Gersten, 2007). For example, students in the treatment condition completed compare–contrast graphic organizers throughout the unit as they encountered each source document, always returning to ones they had previously read or viewed. In small groups, they discussed these comparisons with their peers, and when viewing the documentary, the teacher frequently stopped the video to ask discussion questions that invited comparison with other events and people. Notably, the researchers found that this approach resulted in significantly deeper content comprehension for students with learning disabilities.

Require Students to Summarize in Order to Build Content Knowledge

Handling multiple documents can be quite difficult for students, especially when their prior knowledge is relatively low. In order to build their capacity to perceive connections between and among texts, make sure that students have opportunities to summarize the information. To be clear, we are not talking about summarizing individual readings but, rather, having students summarize the information they have gained from reading multiple texts. For instance, Gil, Bråten, Vidal-Abarca, and Strømsø (2010) used five scientific readings with first-year college students and gave the two groups one of two tasks: to write for summarizing or to write for argument. The first group summarized the information about climate change (the subject of the readings), while the second group stated their personal opinion and required them to use the texts to justify their position. They were scored according to the number of transformations they made, such as paraphrasing and elaborating. In addition, their writing was tabulated according to the ways they integrated the readings, including how many texts they cited and the number of times they switched from one textual citation to another. Somewhat surprisingly, the students in the summary writing condition performed better on the number of transformations and integrations they used.

Writing Moves With Multiple Documents

Teach students the moves writers use when writing across documents, whether for the purposes of summarizing information or for presenting a cogent argument. These writing moves cluster into two categories: writing for transformation and writing for integration (Gil et al., 2010):

Transformational Writing Moves

- Paraphrasing content
- Elaborating using two or more textual sources
- Adding information by drawing on one's own prior knowledge
- Avoiding misconceptions and factual errors

Integration Writing Moves

- Use all of the text sources made available for the task

- Increase the number of switches between texts (e.g., Don't cluster citations so that each section contains evidence drawn from text #2, followed by another section that cites only text #4)

We also like an exercise suggested by Spatz (2011) for getting students ready for writing from multiple sources. Spatz suggests asking students to select a word from a list of ambiguous terms (e.g., *glamorous, masculine, passive, ladylike, aggressive,* and *dominant* to explore gender) and survey several people using the following questions:

- What does X mean? Has it any other meanings that you know of?
- How would you use this word in a sentence?
- Is this a positive or a negative word? In what situation could it possibly seem favorable or unfavorable? (p. 225)

Students then write a short explanatory piece, first addressing the most common meaning among those surveyed (denotation), as well as positive and negative connotations of the word. Students should use direct quotations and paraphrases, cite sources, and summarize.

Extend and Deepen Content Knowledge Through Argument Writing

Gil et al. (2010), the researchers who examined the effects of summary writing and argument writing on multiple document comprehension, had another question: Could it be that a learner's level of prior knowledge influenced how well he or she did? Using a similar approach, they measured each student's prior knowledge about climate change in order to divide them into low-knowledge or high-knowledge groups. This time, the results differed dramatically. The high-knowledge group did much better on the argument writing task than those with low prior knowledge. This has implications for how we foster reading comprehension across documents, as it confirms that when readers have less background knowledge, they need more scaffolded instruction (Fisher & Frey, 2009). In this case, scaffolded instruction comes in part with learning activities that encourage students to summarize across texts before creating arguments to support a position. We feel this is an important point in designing writing tasks. The CCSS laudably call for more writing for argumentation.

But it is essential to understand that argumentation is necessarily built on a strong foundation of content knowledge. Brushing past it will not result in strong writers if students do not already possess a depth of knowledge about the content itself.

Eleventh-grade English teacher Mimi Lin scaffolds her students' ability to engage in writing through the use of a mnemonic designed to aid their ability to apply *topos*, a form of rhetoric used in comparative English essays (Lewis & Ferretti, 2011). *Topoi* are literary pattern analyses that are employed to more deeply understand a work and are commonly evoked in college composition classes. A common one is the ubiquity topos, which relies on the identification of a repeated pattern in a work, such as the use of symbolism. Students in Ms. Lin's class read and discussed several poems by Walt Whitman and Emily Dickinson during a unit on 19th-century American poets. Students selected a theme to explore, such as the poet's treatment of death or love, and developed an essay using a ubiquity topos to shape their argument. Ms. Lin assisted students in identifying the two specific poems they would base their essays on and taught them the THE READER mnemonic to scaffold their writing (Graff, 2003; Lewis & Ferretti, 2011):

- *THE* is a reminder that the essay requires a *thesis*.
- *REA* represents the need for the thesis to be supported by *reasons*.
- *D* stands for the *details* needed, such as quotes and textual evidence.
- *E* is intended to remind students that the details must be *explained* to the reader to support their claims.
- *R* represents the need for a final *review* in the concluding portion of the paper.

"I plan on using this method again for our next comparative essay," Ms. Lin said, continuing:

> It has worked really well, and although I don't want them to remain dependent on this for the entire year, I know it will take some more experiences with analytical writing before they get the hang of it. I'm already seeing evidence that they are looking across both texts and are not just giving me side-by-side comparisons.

Whether writing from one source or many, the task is rarely, if ever, complete in one draft. The process of revising is an essential element of writing and is one that must be cultivated carefully, lest students perceive it as some form of slow-motion torment. No chapter on writing would be complete without a discussion of revising, especially as it applies to involvement of peers and the inclusion of reflective thinking.

Revising: An Essential Writing Practice

The National Writing Project and Nagin (2003) define revision using a gerund:

> In revising, a writer approaches a rough draft with an editorial eye, identifying and deleting extraneous subject matter, focusing the material, determining what needs to be amplified and what needs to be cut… Writers need to learn revision strategies, and teachers can help by modeling the process, showing drafts of their own or someone else's writing and demonstrating how revision can transform and clarify a piece of writing. Students then learn that writing is a continual process of transforming or re-seeing their work. (p. 26)

Unfortunately, in too many classes, revising is really just making the changes the teacher recommended during editing, with little thought beyond minimal compliance. ("I'll just make these changes she wrote on my paper, and then I'll be done with this!")

Lee (2009) interviewed 26 middle and high school English teachers about what they valued in the development of student writing. They spoke of the importance of focusing on a writer's strength and emphasized that good writing was more than accuracy of conventions and mechanics. Teachers in the study said that the usefulness of feedback was contingent upon their students' ability to understand it. Most important, they said, revision was necessary to the development of skilled writers. Lee then analyzed the written feedback of these same teachers on their students' papers and found the following:

- The majority of the feedback focused on errors, mostly about conventions and mechanics.
- They used error codes their students did not understand.
- They assigned a single grade for the initial attempt and did not create opportunities for meaningful revising.

The last finding is disturbing because without revising, students fail to develop the stamina and persistence needed to engage in complex writing. As well, the notion that the teacher alone is the engine for revising is a false one that reinforces the misplaced belief that he or she is the only audience. We have discussed throughout this book that a sense of audience is essential, yet in most classes we don't provide one for them.

Audiences respond. That's what makes them so powerful. We are communicative creatures, and we don't like yelling into a void. It is common practice to provide audiences for very young writers, who read their work from an author's chair to their peers. But that seems to disappear by the intermediate grades. Now we're not advocating for an author's chair in every middle and high school classroom. But we do strongly advocate for putting procedures in place to make the most of peer response.

English teacher Ken Ryu stresses the importance of peer response with his ninth-grade students. "I have always emphasized the importance of audience for their writing, whether it is narrative or expository," he began. "When they start the school year, we begin with discussing the purposes for peer response and how it's different from peer editing." Using a framework described by Simmons (2003), he teaches students about three categories of responses that are useful for their fellow writers:

1. *Playback the text* for the writer by briefly summarizing the main points as you understood them.
2. *Discuss the reader's needs* by alerting the writer to confusions you had as you read the piece.
3. *Identify writer's techniques* you noticed, such as the use of headings, examples, and direct quotes.

"Sometimes they do this face-to-face, but more often lately they do it within a digital environment," Mr. Ryu said. "They insert comments into the margin and code their responses—PT, RN, and WT for the three types of responses I've taught them." Mr. Ryu requires that each writer submit the final version of his or her paper and the marked-up text of the draft. "I get a good perspective on the writer and the reader," he said. "Sometimes the reader makes a really insightful comment that I hadn't even thought of."

Peer response allows writers to gain insight into how their words are understood by others. As a writer, it is difficult to distance oneself from one's words, and peer response, especially the playback, provides novice writers with a means for hearing their words being interpreted by someone else. It reminds both of us of a reading we attended a few years ago by humorist David Sedaris, who at the time was working on his next book. We watched him edit and revise from the stage in real time. Always entertaining, he still managed to mark on his pages when the audience laughed and when it didn't. At times, he tweaked the turn of a phrase and then read it to us again to see if the change improved it. And although we don't expect our own students to become fabulously successful professional writers, we do want them to understand that writing is a form of communication that is often understood somewhat differently from the way the writer intended. Most important, we hope they discover that revising is an ongoing process based on the questions posed, the connections made, and the insights shared by audiences. It is why we continue to write more than 15 years after we wrote our first academic article together.

We return again to the advice of Jago (2002) on the subject of revising. She requires her students to attach a self-assessment of to their final revision:

1. What changes did you make from draft to revision?
2. How did these changes improve your essay?
3. What do you like best about the revised work?
4. What would you continue to work on if you had more time?
5. What else do you want me to know before I read your paper? (p. 108)

The shift in ownership for revising empowers novice writers. Revision, loved or not, becomes less about something the teacher makes me do, and more about assuming responsibility for my efforts. Good writers know they're never done, just that time ran out.

Postwriting Debrief

Major projects, including formal writing assignments, warrant a debriefing. This is a time to gather feedback from students about what worked and what didn't. After the writing assignment is finished, ask students to write "How I wrote this paper," in order to comment on what was easy and difficult and what they did when they were stuck, and to describe the writing environment they worked in. In small groups, students read their papers to one another and discuss the following questions (National Council of Teachers of English, 1996):

1. Were there any similarities among the ways the group members wrote?
2. Were there any major differences among the ways the group members wrote?
3. Did anyone have an especially interesting or unusual approach to writing?
4. What kinds of circumstances did group members agree made it more difficult to write?
5. What circumstances or techniques would you recommend as making writing easier, faster, or more pleasant? (p. 102)

The purpose is twofold: first, to spark metacognitive reflection about the ways in which students help or hurt their own writing processes and, second, to aid the teacher in making formative assessment decisions regarding future teaching.

An Intentional Approach

In the introduction to this book, we introduced a model designed to ensure that students were able to think deeply about the texts they were reading and to produce compositions that reflect that thinking. In a significant part, this is what is required for students to be college and career ready. They will need to do this on a regular basis for their college classes and for their careers. To our thinking, it's important that each aspect of the model is implemented. Students have to be taught how to read closely, using annotations and documenting sources. If they are not, they cannot delve into the meaning of the text or provide a source for their arguments. As part of the instruction required of close reading, teachers need to develop strong text-dependent questions that guide students' thinking. Over time, and with practice, students will begin to ask these types of questions of themselves and their peers as they read.

Students also need time in class to discuss the texts that they read. Complex texts require interrogation, and that can be facilitated with peer interaction. Adult readers do this all of the time. We like to talk about what we've read. We share examples, tidbits, and anecdotes from the various texts we read with the people we encounter. How many conversations have you had with another person that started with, "Have you read" or

"According to"? It's part of our culture and patterns of interaction. We're social animals, and one of the ways we socialize is through the texts we've read.

It's also important to be intentional about writing and demanding that students write using evidence from the texts they've read. It's not enough to simply tell students to use evidence; they have to be taught to do so. This starts with a prompt that includes information about the topic, the audience, and the rhetorical structure or genre to be produced. It's this backward planning design that allows teachers to develop lessons that work. With the end in mind, we invite you to lead your students to higher levels of achievement.

REFERENCES

Adler, M.J., & Van Doren, C. (1972). *How to read a book* (Rev. ed.). New York, NY: Touchstone. (Original work published 1940)

Allington, R.L. (2002). You can't learn much from books you can't read. *Educational Leadership, 60*(3), 16–19.

Alvermann, D.E. (1991). The discussion web: A graphic aid for learning across the curriculum. *The Reading Teacher, 45*(2), 92–99.

American Psychological Association. (2010). *Publication manual of the American Psychological Association* (6th ed.). Washington, DC: Author.

Applebee, A.N., Langer, J.A., Nystrand, M., & Gamoran, A. (2003). Discussion-based approaches to developing understanding: Classroom instruction and student performance in middle and high school English. *American Educational Research Journal, 40*(3), 685–730.

Aronson, E., Bridgeman, D., & Geffner, R. (1978). Interdependent interactions and prosocial behavior. *Journal of Research and Development in Education, 12*(1), 16–27.

Baron, D. (2007). Using text-based protocols: Rendering the text. *Principal Leadership: High School Edition, 7*(7), 46–49.

Beach, R. (2012). Constructing digital learning commons in the literacy classroom. *Journal of Adolescent & Adult Literacy, 55*(5), 448–451.

Bereiter, C., & Scardamalia, M. (1982). From conversation to composition: The role of instruction in a developmental process. In R. Glaser (Ed.), *Advances in instructional psychology* (Vol. 2, pp. 1–64). Hillsdale, NJ: Erlbaum.

Bråten, I., & Strømsø, H.I. (2010). When law students read multiple documents about global warming: Examining the role of topic-specific beliefs about the nature of knowledge and knowing. *Instructional Science, 38*, 635–657.

Bromley, K.D. (1985). Précis writing and outlining to enhance content learning. *The Reading Teacher, 38*(4), 406–411.

Burke, J. (2002). *Tools for thought: Graphic organizers for your classroom*. Portsmouth, NH: Heinemann.

Cazden, C.B. (1988). *Classroom discourse: The language of teaching and learning*. Portsmouth, NH: Heinemann.

Chall, J.S., & Dale, E. (1995). *Manual for the new Dale-Chall readability formula*. Cambridge, MA: Brookline.

Chin, C., & Osborne, J. (2010). Students' questions and discursive interaction: Their impact on argumentation during collaborative group discussions in science. *Journal of Research in Science Teaching, 47*(7), 883–908.

Coleman, D., & Pimentel, S. (2012). *Revised publishers' criteria for the Common Core State Standards in English language arts and literacy, grades 3–12*. Retrieved from www.corestandards.org/assets/Publishers_Criteria_for_3-12.pdf

Cunningham, J. (1982). Generating interactions between schemata and text. In J.A. Niles & L.A. Harris (Eds.), *New inquiries in reading research and instruction* (pp. 42–47). Washington, DC: National Reading Conference.

Daniels, H. (2002). *Literature circles: Voice and choice in book clubs and reading groups* (2nd ed.). York, ME: Stenhouse.

Davey, B. (1983). Think-aloud: Modeling the cognitive processes of reading comprehension. *Journal of Reading, 27*(1), 44–47.

Duffy, G.G. (2003). *Explaining reading: A resource for teaching concepts, skills, and strategies.* New York, NY: Guilford.

Espin, C.A., Cevasco, J., van den Broek, P., Baker, S., & Gersten, R. (2007). History as narrative: The nature and quality of historical understanding for students with LD. *Journal of Learning Disabilities, 40*(2), 174–182.

Fisher, D., & Frey, N. (2009). *Background knowledge: The missing piece of the comprehension puzzle.* Portsmouth, NH: Heinemann.

Fisher, D., & Frey, N. (2013). *Common Core English language arts in a PLC at work, grades 6–8 and 9–12.* Bloomington, IN: Solution Tree.

Fisher, D., Frey, N., & Rothenberg, C. (2008). *Content-area conversations: How to plan discussion-based lessons for diverse language learners.* Alexandria, VA: ASCD.

Flesch, R. (1948). A new readability yardstick. *Journal of Applied Psychology, 32*(3), 221–233.

Flower, L. (1990a). Negotiating academic discourse. In L. Flower, V. Stein, J. Ackerman, M.J. Kantz, K. McCormick, & W.C. Peck (Eds.), *Reading-to-write: Exploring a cognitive and social process* (pp. 221–252). New York, NY: Oxford University Press.

Flower, L. (1990b). Studying cognition in context. In L. Flower, V. Stein, J. Ackerman, M.J. Kantz, K. McCormick, & W.C. Peck (Eds.), *Reading-to-write: Exploring a cognitive and social process* (pp. 3–32). New York, NY: Oxford University Press.

Flower, L. (1993). *Problem-solving strategies for writing* (4th ed.). San Diego, CA: Harcourt.

Frey, N., & Fisher, D. (2013). *Rigorous reading: 5 access points for comprehending complex texts.* Thousand Oaks, CA: Corwin.

Frey, N., Fisher, D., & Gonzalez, A. (2010). *Literacy 2.0: Reading and writing in 21st century classrooms.* Bloomington, IN: Solution Tree.

Frey, N., Fisher, D., & Gonzalez, A. (2013). *Teaching with tablets.* Alexandria, VA: ASCD Arias.

Frey, N., Fisher, D., & Hernandez, T. (2003). "What's the gist?" Summary writing for struggling adolescent writers. *Voices from the Middle, 11*(2), 43–49.

Fry, E. (2002). Readability versus leveling. *The Reading Teacher, 56*(3), 288.

Gil, L., Bråten, I., Vidal-Abarca, E., & Strømsø, H.I. (2010). Summary versus argument tasks when working with multiple documents: Which is better for whom? *Contemporary Educational Psychology, 35*(3), 157–173.

Goldman, S.R. (2004). Cognitive aspects of constructing meaning through and across multiple texts. In N. Shuart-Faris & D. Bloome (Eds.), *Uses of intertextuality in classroom and educational research* (pp. 317–351). Greenwich, CT: Information Age.

Goldman, S.R., & Rakestraw, J.A. (2000). Structural aspects of constructing meaning from text. In M.L. Kamil, P. Mosenthal, P.D. Pearson, & R. Barr (Eds.), *Handbook of reading research* (Vol. 3, pp. 311–335). Mahwah, NJ: Erlbaum.

Graff, G. (2003). *Clueless in academe: How schooling obscures the life of the mind.* New Haven, CT: Yale University Press.

Graff, G., & Birkenstein, C. (2010). *They say, I say: The moves that matter in academic writing* (2nd ed.). New York, NY: W. W. Norton & Company.

Gunning, T. (2003). The role of readability in today's classroom. *Topics in Language Disorders, 23*(3), 175–189.

Harris, R. (2010, November 22). *Evaluating Internet research sources*. VirtualSalt. Retrieved from www.virtualsalt.com/evalu8it.htm

Hattie, J. (2009). *Visible learning: A synthesis of over 800 meta-analyses relating to achievement*. New York, NY: Routledge.

Hayes, D.P., Wolfer, L.T., & Wolfe, M.F. (1996). Sourcebook simplification and its relation to the decline in SAT-Verbal scores. *American Educational Research Journal, 33*(2), 489–508.

Headquarters of the Department of the Army. (2007). *Army leadership: Army regulation 600–100* [Publishing Directorate]. Washington, DC: Author. Retrieved from www.apd.army.mil/pdffiles/r600_100.pdf

Howard, R.M., & Robillard, A.E. (Eds.). (2008). *Pluralizing plagiarism: Identities, contexts, pedagogies*. Portsmouth, NH: Boynton/Cook.

Ivey, G., & Johnston, P. (2013). Engagement with young adult literature: Outcomes and processes. *Reading Research Quarterly, 48*(3), 255–275.

Jago, C. (2002). *Cohesive writing: Why concept is not enough*. Portsmouth, NH: Heinemann.

Kagan, L., Kagan, M., & Kagan, S. (1997). *Cooperative learning structures for teambuilding*. San Clemente, CA: Kagan.

Kennedy, R.F. (1968, April 4). *Statement by Senator Robert F. Kennedy on the death of the Reverend Martin Luther King, April 4, 1968* [Speech]. National Archives and Records Administration ARC Identifier 194037. Retrieved from research.archives.gov/description/194037

Kobayashi, K. (2005). What limits the encoding effect of note-taking? A meta-analytic examination. *Contemporary Educational Psychology, 30*(2), 242–262.

Koslin, B.L., Zeno, S., & Koslin, S. (1987). *The DRP: An effective measure of reading*. New York, NY: College Entrance Examination Board.

Kurland, D. (1994). *I know what it says...What does it mean? Critical skills for critical reading*. Belmont, CA: Wadsworth.

Lee, D.Y.W. (2001). Genres, registers, text types, domains, and styles: Clarifying the concepts and navigating a path through the BNC jungle. *Language Learning and Technology, 5*(3), 37–72.

Lee, I. (2009). Ten mismatches between teachers' beliefs and written feedback practice. *ELT Journal, 63*(1), 13–22.

Leu, D.J., & Kinzer, C.K. (2000). The convergence of literacy instruction with networked technologies for information and communication. *Reading Research Quarterly, 35*(1), 108–127.

Lewis, W.E., & Ferretti, R.P. (2011). Topoi and literary interpretation: The effects of a critical reading and writing intervention on high school students' analytic literary essays. *Contemporary Educational Psychology, 36*(4), 334–354.

McQuade, D., & McQuade, C. (2006). *Seeing & writing 3*. Boston, MA: Bedford/St. Martin's.

Michaels, S., O'Connor, C., & Resnick, L.B. (2008). Deliberative discourse idealized and realized: Accountable talk in the classroom and in civic life. *Studies in Philosophy and Education, 27*(4), 283–297.

Michaels, S., O'Connor, M.C., Hall, M.W., & Resnick, L.B. (2010). *Accountable talk sourcebook: For classroom conversation that works* (v.3.1). University of Pittsburgh

Institute for Learning. Retrieved from ifl.lrdc.pitt.edu/ifl/index.php/download/index/ats/

Mitchell, S. (2001). What is this thing called argument? In R. Andrews & S. Mitchell (Eds.), *Essays in argument* (pp. 21–34). London, UK: Middlesex University Press.

Monte-Sano, C., & De La Paz, S. (2012). Using writing tasks to elicit adolescents' historical reasoning. *Journal of Literacy Research, 44*(3), 273–299.

National Assessment Governing Board. (2010). *Writing framework for the 2011 National Assessment of Educational Progress.* Washington, DC: Author. Retrieved from www.nagb.org/content/nagb/assets/documents/publications/frameworks/writing-2011.pdf

National Council of Teachers of English. (1996). *Motivating writing in middle school.* Urbana, IL: Author.

National Governors Association Center for Best Practices & Council of Chief State School Officers. (2010a). *Common Core State Standards for English language arts and literacy in history/social studies, science, and technical subjects.* Washington DC: Authors. Retrieved from www.corestandards.org/assets/CCSSI_ELA%20Standards.pdf

National Governors Association Center for Best Practices & Council of Chief State School Officers. (2010b). *Common Core State Standards for English language arts and literacy in history/social studies, science, and technical subjects: Appendix A: Research supporting key elements of the standards and glossary of key terms.* Washington, DC: Authors. Retrieved from www.corestandards.org/assets/Appendix_A.pdf

National Writing Project & Nagin, C. (2003). *Because writing matters: Improving student writing in our schools.* San Francisco, CA: Jossey-Bass.

Newkirk, T. (2011). *The art of slow reading: Six time-honored practices for engagement.* Portsmouth, NH: Heinemann.

Nystrand, M., Wu, L.L., Gamoran, A., Zeiser, S., & Long, D. (2003). Questions in time: Investigating the structure and dynamics of unfolding classroom discourse. *Discourse Processes, 35*(2), 135–196.

Oliver, E. (1995). The writing quality of seventh, ninth, and eleventh graders, and college freshmen: Does rhetorical specification in writing prompts make a difference? *Research in the Teaching of English, 29*(4), 422–450.

Palincsar, A.S., & Brown, A.L. (1984). Reciprocal teaching of comprehension-fostering and comprehension-monitoring activities. *Cognition and Instruction, 1*(2), 117–175.

Perfetti, C.A., Rouet, J.-F., & Britt, M.A. (1999). Toward a theory of documents representation. In H. van Oostendorp & S.R. Goldman (Eds.), *The construction of mental representations during reading* (pp. 88–108). Mahwah, NJ: Erlbaum.

Pilgreen, J.L. (2000). *The SSR handbook: How to organize and manage a sustained silent reading program.* Portsmouth, NH: Boynton/Cook.

Poe, E.A. (1988). *Marginalia.* Charlottesville: University of Virginia Press. (Original work published 1844)

Quindlen, A. (2001, September 27). "A Quilt of a Country." *Newsweek.* Retrieved from www.newsweek.com/quilt-country-151869

RAND Reading Study Group. (2002). *Reading for understanding: Toward an R&D program in reading comprehension.* Retrieved from www.rand.org/pubs/monograph_reports/MR1465.html

Roberts, T., & Billings, L. (2012). *Teaching critical thinking: Using seminars for 21st century literacy.* Larchmont, NY: Eye on Education.

Roosevelt, F.D. (1941, January 6). Address to Congress. *Congressional Record, 1941* (Vol. 87, Pt. 1). Retrieved from www.fdrlibrary.marist.edu/fourfreedoms

Rosenblatt, L.M. (1938/1978). *The reader, the text, the poem: The transactional theory of the literary work.* Carbondale, IL: Southern Illinois University Press.

Rosenblatt, L.M. (1995). *Literature as exploration* (5th ed.). New York, NY: Modern Language Association.

Sanders, T.J.M., & Schilperoord, J. (2006). Text structure as a window on the cognition of writing: How text analysis provides insights in writing products and writing processes. In C.A. MacArthur, S. Graham, & J. Fitzgerald (Eds.), *Handbook of writing research* (pp. 386–402). New York, NY: Guilford.

Shanahan, T. (2013). *Meeting the common core challenge: Planning close reading.* Retrieved from sites.google.com/site/tscommoncore/home/close-reading

Simmons, J. (2003). Responders are taught, not born. *Journal of Adolescent & Adult Literacy, 46*(8), 684–693.

Smith, D., Stenner, A.J., Horabin, I., & Smith, M. (1989). *The Lexile scale in theory and practice: Final report.* Washington, DC: MetaMetrics. [ERIC Document Reproduction Service No. ED 307577]

Solomon, A. (2012). *Far from the tree: Parents, children, and the search for identity.* New York, NY: Scribner.

Spatt, B. (2011). *Writing from sources* (8th ed.). Boston, MA: Bedford/St. Martin's.

Stahl, N.A., King, J.R., & Henk, W.A. (1991). Enhancing students' notetaking through training and evaluation. *Journal of Reading, 34*(8), 614–622.

Toulmin, S.E. (1954). *The uses of argument.* Cambridge, UK: Cambridge Press.

Tufte, E. (2006). *Beautiful evidence.* Cheshire, CT: Graphics.

U.S. Congress. (2009). *Circular 92: Copyright law of the United States and related laws contained in Title 17 of the United States code.* 111th Cong., 1st sess., 2009. Washington, DC: U.S. Printing Office. Retrieved from www.copyright.gov/title17/

Wellington, J J., & Osborne, J.A. (2001). *Language and literacy in science education.* Philadelphia, PA: Open University.

Wikipedia. (n.d.). *Plagiarism.* Retrieved from en.wikipedia.org/wiki/Plagiarism

Wineburg, S.S. (1991). On the reading of historical texts: Notes on the breach between school and academy. *American Educational Research Journal, 28*(3) 495–519.

Zhang, S., Duke, N.K., & Jiménez, L.M. (2011). The WWWDOT approach to improving students' critical evaluation of websites. *The Reading Teacher, 65*(2), 150–158.

LITERATURE CITED

Alexie, S. (1994). *The Lone Ranger and Tonto fistfight in heaven.* New York, NY: Harper Perennial.

Baldwin, J. (1965). Sonny's blues. In *Going to meet the man* (pp.101–141). New York, NY: Dial.

Carroll, L. (1999). *Through the looking-glass and what Alice found there.* Mineola, NY: Dover. (Original work published 1872)

Cisneros, S. (1991). *Woman Hollering Creek: And other stories.* New York, NY: Random House.

Lee, H. (1960/2002). *To kill a mockingbird.* New York, NY: Harper Perennial.

London, J. (1906/2003). *The call of the wild* and *White Fang*. New York, NY: Barnes and Noble Classics.

McCourt, F. (2006). *Teacher man: A memoir*. New York: Scribner.

McCrae, J. (1915). *In Flanders fields*. Retrieved from en.wikipedia.org/wiki/In_Flanders_Fields

Murphy, J. (1995). *The great fire*. New York, NY: Scholastic.

Sheinkin, S. (2012). *Bomb: The race to build—and steal—the world's most dangerous weapon*. New York, NY: Roaring Book.

Stalin, J. (1954). *Works* (Vol. 11). Moscow, Russia: Foreign Languages Publishing House.

Vonnegut, K. (1998). *Cat's cradle*. New York, NY: Dell.

INDEX

Note. Page numbers followed by *f* or *t* indicate figures or tables, respectively.

citations: standards for, 49, 50*t*; style guides for, 90

clarifying, 99

classroom discussion. *See* Discussions

classroom instruction, 75–76

classroom routines, 101–109

close reading, 30; building capacity through, 41–49; of complex texts, 34–62

closing questions, 114

Coleman, D., 97

collaboration, 99

collaborative annotation, 73–74

College and Career Readiness (CCR) Anchor Standards, 51–55, 52*t*; for Craft and Structure, 52*t*, 53–54; for Integration of Knowledge and Ideas, 52*t*; for Key Ideas and Details, 52*t*, 52–53; Standard 1 in Speaking and Listening, 102

Common Core, 35

Common Core State Standards (CCSS), 16, 21, 49, 132, 139–140; essential skills for achieving goals set forth by, 63–64; for writing, 9. *See also* College and Career Readiness (CCR) Anchor Standards

complex texts: close reading of, 34–62; reading, 40–41; selection of, 35–41

comprehension of multiple texts, 132–133

confusions, 46

content analysis, 37

content instruction, 68–73

content knowledge: building, 138; extending and deepening, 139–141

content scraping, 85

contextualizing, 132

conversations: annotations as, 65; recommended moves, 98–99; text discussions, 46

copyright, 84

Copyright Act, 84

Core Standards for the English language arts, 21

Council of Chief State School Officers (CCSSO), 9, 16, 34–35, 37, 102, 132

craft: CCR Anchor Standards, 52*t*, 53–54; examining, 47

Cunningham, J., 80, 124

D

Dale, E., 36

Daniels, H., 41, 112

Davey, B., 40

De La Paz, S., 121, 133

Declaration of Independence, 29

Degrees of Reading Power, 36

Dialogue approach, 119, 120*t*

Dickinson, E., 140

digital collaborative annotation, 74

digital sources, 132

Diigo, 74, 81, 82

discourse, academic, 115

discussion roundtables, 105–107, 106*f*

discussion webs, 109–112; final set of instructions for, 110; graphic aid for, 109–110, 111*f*

discussions: argumentation in, 109–115; Carousel routine, 103–104; classroom routines to promote, 101–109; conversational moves in, 98–99; essential teacher dispositions for, 94; evidence in, 7–33, 93–115; follow-up probes for, 96; of imagery, 67; Initiate-Respond-Evaluate (IRE) discourse, 95; keeping channels open, 99; keeping everyone together, 99; leading, 94–95; literature circles, 112; meaningful, 115–116; preparing for, 63–92; as productive group work, 105; Socratic seminars, 112–115; strengthening student capacity to use evidence in, 104–109; sustained student-led, 104–105; text-based, 46, 94–95, 102–103; text-based questions to drive, 95–101; text types for, 20–32; textual evidence in, 3*f*, 3–4

Documents Model framework, 133

Duffy, G.G., 88, 126

Duke, N.K., 32

E

Eisenhower, D.D., 42, 44*f*, 45*f*

English language arts (ELA): example

U.S. Constitution, 107
U.S. history, 122

V

van den Broek, P., 137
Van Doren, C., 64
verifying, 99
vertical lines in the margin, 64
Vidal-Abarca, E., 138
visual supports, 38
Vonnegut, K., 37

W

The Washington Post, 91
Wellington, J.J., 136
Whitman, W., 140
Wineburg, S.S., 31, 132
Wolfe, M.F., 34
Wolfer, L.T., 34
words and phrases: circling of key words or phrases, 65; impact on meaning, 59; text-dependent questions about, 55–56
writing: argument, 16–20, 18*f*, 21, 22*t*, 139–141; as constructive process, 116–117, 117*f*; evidence in, 3*f*, 3–4, 7–33; explanatory, 13–16, 21, 23*t*; framing for reluctant writers, 129–131; GIST, 80; integration writing moves, 138–139; intentional approach to, 144–145; in margins, 65, 74; across multiple texts, 131–132, 138–139; narrative, 10–13, 21, 24*t*; persuasive, 16–20, 18*f*, 25; postwriting debrief, 143–144; précis writing, 123, 124–125; preparing for, 63–92; THE READER mnemonic for scaffolding, 140; reading-to-write strategies, 118–119, 120*t*; scaffolding, 140; skilled, 121; from sources, 116–145; standards for, 9; summary, 80–81, 123–124, 126*t*; text types, 20–32; textual evidence in, 3*f*, 3–4; transformational writing moves, 138. *See also* Annotation
writing about, 116
Writing Anchor Standard 8, 132
writing assignments, 117–118, 122; basic components of, 120–123; effective, 120–123; examples, 122; questions answered for, 121
writing from, 116
writing narrative, 10–13; standards for, 21, 24*t*
writing prompts, 122
writing questions, 74
writing responses, 142
writing tasks, 122
writing to inform: standards for, 21, 23*t*
written sources, 79–81
Wu, L.L., 95
WWWDOT mnemonic, 32

Z

Zeiser, S., 95
Zeno, S., 36
Zhang, S., 32